To Dr. Goyert,

Thank you for your interest in my services. I would enjoy the opportunity to work with you.

Best Regards,

[signature]

2/21/95

THE

LIFE INSURANCE

FIASCO

HOW TO AVOID IT

THE

LIFE INSURANCE

FIASCO

HOW TO AVOID IT

PETER C. KATT

Dolphin Publishing
West Bloomfield, Michigan

Additional copies of this book may be ordered through bookstores or by sending $19.95 plus $3.50 for postage and handling to: Publishers Distribution Service, 121 East Front Street, Suite 203, Traverse City, MI 49684.
1-800-345-0096

Copyright © 1992 by Peter C. Katt

Publisher's Cataloging-in-Publication Data

Katt, Peter C., 1945-
      The life insurance fiasco: how to avoid it / by Peter C. Katt.
           p.   cm.
      Includes Index.
      ISBN 0-9629957-0-3 (hc.)
      ISBN 0-9629957-1-1 (pbk.)
      1. Insurance, Life - United States. 2. Life Insurance Commis-
      sions. I. Title

HG8771.K38   1992
368.3'--dc20   91-72305

Manufactured in the United States of America

For my wife — Karen

A loving and loved kindred spirit

For Mother

Nuturing — Understanding — Love

For my daughter — Erinn

Ahead — a lifetime of discovery and experience

ACKNOWLEDGMENTS

I have had the help and encouragement of many wonderful people. I would like to thank:

Con Hitchock, an attorney with Public Citizen. This consumer oriented organization has represented me in legal battles with the Michigan Insurance Bureau;

Maria Crawford Scott, editor of the *American Association of Individual Investors (AAII) Journal*. Maria, for good or bad, was the impetus for this book. She first asked me for an article, then a regular column, which has now resulted in this book;

Jean Henrich, an assistant editor for the *AAII Journal*. Anyone who has written a book knows the importance of a good copy editor. Without destroying my ego, Jean improved my manuscript resulting in an efficient writing style. I wouldn't write a book without her;

Jerrold Jenkins, President of Publishers Distribution Service. This company has guided me in independent publishing without hassle. And, Alex Moore for fulfilling Jerrold's promises;

Jane Bryant Quinn, syndicated columnist. Almost alone among media stars, Jane has the courage to take sides and expose, as she sees it, financial services that are consumer rip-offs and those that are consumer friendly. Jane has written several columns that have been very generous in explaining my services and battles with the life insurance industry and regulators;

Glenn Daily, a fellow fee-for-service life insurance adviser and author. Glenn and I have the advantage on initially disagreeing about nearly everything. This requires us to better develop our arguments. This process has strengthened each of us professionally and contributed to a strong personal friendship;

H. Lynn Hopewell, a fee-for-service investment and financial adviser. Given Lynn's reputation, I am flattered and appreciative of his kind comments about my book; and

Reed H. Nelson, my father-in-law. Need I say more.

CONTENTS

INTRODUCTION

This book has two principal goals. One is to describe, in partisan terms, the serious problems consumers face when dealing with a system for buying life insurance that is nearly exclusively motivated by the large commissions agents earn from its sale. The other principal goal is to describe two alternative systems now available to consumers for their life insurance planning and purchases that avoid the negative aspects of the commission-motivated system.

I am partisan in my approach to this subject because I am a participant, and a pioneer, in one of the two alternative systems. I am a fee-for-service life insurance adviser, a service described in this book. Basically, fee-for-service life insurance advisers are compensated directly by their clients rather than by the life insurance company via commissions. This creates a relationship ensuring objectivity and based on trust and confidence. In addition our clients are given access to wholesale costs for their life insurance purchases by the recommendation of policies that pay no commission.

The other alternative I describe as a direct-response system. In this system, consumers rationally determine the amount and type of life insurance they wish to purchase (instructions on how this is done constitute a major portion of this book) without a life insurance salesman's pressure tactics and contact directly one of the two life insurance companies offering no-commission life insurance policies. Under each system consumers will experience enormous savings.

Because of the objective advice given by fee-for-service life insurance advisers or inner-directed purchases of life insurance by consumers using the methods described in this book, consumers can avoid life insurance salesmen whose purchase recommendations frequently lack a rational basis. This criticism is supported by the dismal cancellation rate for permanent policies. Industry studies indicate that half of all whole life policies purchased will be cancelled within seven years.

Tremendous interest is currently focused on the life insurance industry because of the well publicized severe financial difficulties of a half-dozen, or so, life insurance companies. This has created great hardship for the policyholders of these companies and has led to a loss of consumer confidence in the life insurance industry. But these problems will be corrected because the industry knows what has caused them. Of much greater importance are the staggering losses consumers suffer due to this high policy cancellation rate. Such cancellations can only be explained by the failure of the commission-based system for selling life insurance to consistently make appropriate purchase recommendations. These policy cancellation losses are due to the very high distributions costs associated with the sale of life insurance. The distribution costs, which are almost entirely commissions paid to the selling agent and his general agent, are 100% and more of the first year premium, 10% and more of premiums for another four to nine years and 3% and more thereafter.

A Life Insurance Marketing and Research Association, Inc. (LIMRA) 1990 long-term whole life cancellation study found that, of the policies studied, 54% had been cancelled within the first seven years.

Over the past few years new life insurance premiums have been approximately $10 billion annually. It is difficult to apply the LIMRA study to this new annual premium sales figure because it includes all types of life insurance while the study only reviewed whole life policies. Also, there are other factors that make a direct correlation unwise. However, some life insurance critics believe that the early cancellation of life insurance policies costs consumers nearly $1.0 billion each year. Of course, what the consumer loses the agent has gained in form of commissions earned. Selling is an art, and commissions are the engine that drives many commercial relations. However, when so many consumers commit such obvious economic suicide by so quickly cancelling their policies, too many agents are doing a lousy job. While our attention is focused on the dramatic news of life insurance company financial woes, these consumer losses due to policy cancellation are the industry's dirty little secret.

Dirty secrets aside, this book should not be interpreted as advocating an overhaul of the entire commission-motivated system for selling life insurance. As a strong advocate of free markets, I would reject any attempt (as impossible as it would be) to change the overall structure of the present commission-motivated system. In fact, the commission-motivated system for selling life insurance is useful for the vast majority of life insurance consumers, who are apathetic. Agents must develop creative solicitation skills and be able to manipulate the engagement in such a manner to win a sale. Without these attributes developed by agents, many apathetic consumers wouldn't own any personal life insurance. With life insurance sales in 1992 expected to produce new annual premiums of approximately $10 billion, these commission-motivated agents have a vast population of apathetic consumers to conquer. This may be faint praise of the commission-motivated system for selling life insurance, but the role this system plays for apathetic consumers should not be underestimated.

Direct-response and fee-for-service life insurance advisers are the alternatives from which informed consumers may choose. I am very willing to abide by what the market decides concerning these alternatives without seeking the overhaul of the commission-motivated system through government regulations. As a matter of fact, as described in Chapter Four, the commission-dominated system for the marketing and selling of life insurance presently has certain market restraints the industry not only approves of, but has a good deal of influence over.

Readers might wonder why this book should be written by a participant in the life insurance business. Unfortunately, this book couldn't be written by an academician or consumer advocate. Research on the part of the academician or controlled anger on the part of the consumer advocate is not adequate to understand the issues in the trenches. Only a life insurance veteran can understand the behavior of life insurance agents in their relationships with customers.

We live in a world of euphemisms where image and claims dominate, but are poor substitutes for substance and performance (paraphrased from Richard Schickel, a movie critic for Time Magazine). Just as a mountain lake scene captured on film depicts a tranquil setting, the life insurance industry spends heavily to instill a sense of tranquillity and consumer confidence ("get a piece of the Rock," "The Quiet Company," etc.). The reality, however is quite different. Within the trees and below the water surface of this mountain lake is a fierce battle for survival. And the reality of the life insurance industry is very different from the advertised image. Since 1979 I have observed the bifurcation between the image the life insurance industry has created for its agents and their very different performance on a day-to-day basis with consumers.

The criticisms leveled at the life insurance industry and its agents are supported primarily by my first-hand experiences gained as a participant, some of which are described here.

However, an early reader of my manuscript pointed out that I run the risk of alienating my readers if I load this book up with too many specific negative examples of life insurance agents' behavior to demonstrate larger points. On the other hand, I wanted to provide readers with a vivid understanding of the problems within the life insurance industry. To satisfy both positions, I have for the most part described specific experiences with life insurance agents in appendices in the back of this book. Those readers who are interested in what led me to my conclusions concerning life insurance agents' behavior can read these appendices. I strongly recommend that if you are interested in these experiences, you read these appendices as they are mentioned. If they are read as the final sections of the book their relevance will be diminished.

It was suggested that I eliminate the negative aspects or provide a more "fair" presentation of the commission-motivated system for selling life insurance in this book. In my view, such advice misses the point of the book, which is advocacy. Removing the negative slant in order to appeal to a larger number of consumers is not only questionable, it's undesirable. Constructing a benign amalgamation of competing views would have left this book's target audience, astute consumers, unable to discern critical differences between the commission-motivated approach being attacked and the direct-response and fee-for-service approaches being championed.

Also, I take the position that the serious problems associated with the commission-motivated system for selling life insurance are an integral part of that system. There are differences between agents as to how they conduct themselves with customers, but these differences are of degree, not of kind. It is the system itself that I attack. Therefore, viewing the commission-motivated system with neutrality and only recommending that consumers avoid agents who are explicitly selfish would create confusion. The real issue is that the system has inherent and unavoidable conflicts of interest regardless of the quality of the agent you may choose, or more precisely the quality of the agent who chooses you.

The Life Insurance Fiasco: How To Avoid It is for astute consumers who wish to take an active role in their life insurance planning. Webster defines astute as shrewdly discerning. I believe that astute consumers have the ability and motivation to gain an advantage over commercial relationships established to service apathetic consumers. The established methods for the marketing and selling of life insurance are designed with apathetic consumers in mind. Astute consumers pay a heavy price for staying in this established system.

The first part of this book is intended to alert astute consumers to the serious problems associated with the commission-motivated system for the marketing and selling of life insurance. Understanding these problems is the precursor to developing the motivation for taking charge of your own life insurance planning. The second part of this book provides instructions for astute and motivated consumers ready to act on their desire to take charge of their life insurance planning.

This book is written as simply as possible. It is not a scholarly treatise or intended generally to be a research source on life insurance. In fact, I wish it could have been much shorter. It is based on the theory that you want to know what time it is, not how to repair a watch. For readers who would like a more thorough explanation of life insurance and particularly low-load, no-commission life insurance policies, I recommend Glenn S. Daily's *The Individual Investors Guide to Low-Load Insurance Products*, published by International Publishing Corporation. Mr. Daily's book is an excellent source of information on the various forms of low-load life and disability insurance policies and low-load annuity policies.

In order to keep this information up-to-date, you may subscribe to the *Astute Life Insurance Consumer's Advisory* newsletter, published annually for a subscription fee of $9.00. This newsletter will bring not only the material presented in this book up-to-date, but will advise you of other life insurance developments that may be important for you to know. Subscribing to the *Astute Life Insurance Consumer's Advisory* is particularly recommended for consumers who intend to do their own life insurance planning and purchases because the material presented in this book will inevitably become outdated. For example, other companies may begin offering no- commission policies on a direct basis. And Congress frequently changes tax laws that affect life insurance planning. If you are interested in this newsletter, send a note requesting this newsletter along with a check for $9.00 to: Dolphin Publishing Co., P.O. Box 250752, W. Bloomfield, MI 48325.

I don't claim that the methods recommended for life insurance planning are the best or only methods. Further, the no-commission life insurance policies being recommended, on a direct basis, may not prove to be the most economical life insurance policies you could buy. I do stand by the logic and rationale for the recommendations that are made and expect to be held to a reasonable standard for professional judgment.

A suggestion for reading this book: Read it all the way through first without getting lost in the specific issues or calculations. You may find that material in later parts of the book will give you a better total picture that may aid in your utilization of specific methods and recommendations.

THE

LIFE INSURANCE

FIASCO

HOW TO AVOID IT

CHAPTER ONE

THE TWO BASIC TYPES OF LIFE INSURANCE

Describing the two basic types of life insurance is necessary at the outset of this book for readers unfamiliar with the differences between the two, and those who generally have very little knowledge about life insurance.

In order to keep this basic explanation of term and permanent life insurance as simple as possible it is presented in bare-bones fashion. Hopefully, it will give you a foundation for understanding later chapters, which unavoidably are a little more complicated.

The two basic types of life insurance sold are term and permanent. Term insurance provides a death benefit and nothing more. There is no policy equity or cash value. Permanent insurance, on the other hand, generates a policy cash value.

There are only three basic pricing components to a life insurance policy. They are:

1. Cost of paying death claims;
2. Expenses; and
3. Investment return on premiums held until death claims are paid.

Term and permanent insurance policy expenses are a major topic of this book. For now they have been ignored to facilitate a better basic understanding of the differences between these two basic types of life insurance policies. For the same reason, the investment component relevant to term insurance has also been ignored.

The major pricing component of term insurance is the insurance company's obligation to pay a specified death benefit, which is known as the mortality cost or the cost of insurance. One of the raw materials within the life insurance industry is the knowledge about the statistical chances of the insured dying during any particular year. This knowledge is condensed and is represented by the cost per $1,000 of death benefit. Cost per $1,000 is the basic unit cost within the life insurance industry.

The major pricing component of term insurance is charging enough premium to pay anticipated death claims. For example, if the statistical chance of dying this year, based on age and health condition, is one in 500, the pure mortality cost of the annual premium is $2.00 per $1,000 of death benefit, which is a 500 to 1 ratio. Therefore, for a $100,000 policy, the pure cost of insurance would be $200.00 ($2.00 per $1,000 of death benefit, or $2.00 x 100).

As the insured gets older, one year at a time, the chances of dying increase. Therefore, the annual term insurance premium increases each year as well. Exhibit 1-1 demonstrates this relationship:

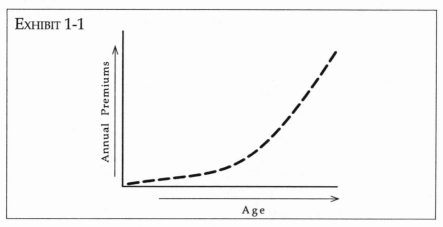

EXHIBIT 1-1

Annual Premiums

Age

But term insurance premiums aren't quite this simple. If they were, most insurance companies would have nearly the same premium pricing. Company investment results, policy expenses and competition in the marketplace have a significant influence on term insurance premium pricing. Therefore, term insurance costs have a relatively wide range.

Currently, one of the most popular forms of term insurance is a policy in which the premium remains level for a specified period of time, such as five years. Rather than increasing the premium every year, these level term policies charge an average cost of insurance each year over the specified period the premium remains level.

Permanent life insurance is known as whole life, universal life, interest-sensitive whole life and variable life. In simplest terms, term insurance is pay as you go, while permanent insurance is priced about three to eight times higher than the initial term insurance premium to create a policy surplus.

The policy surplus, known as the cash value, earns compound interest from the insurance company's many investments and is not currently taxable to the insured.

The surplus accumulates on a compounding, tax-deferred basis and is part of the death benefit. The difference between the total death benefit and the surplus is the amount of pure insurance benefit, or the risk portion of the policy. As Exhibit 1-2 demonstrates, the risk portion of the policy decreases each year as the surplus builds. For example, if the policy's death benefit is $100,000, and the policy's cash value (surplus) is $5,000, the

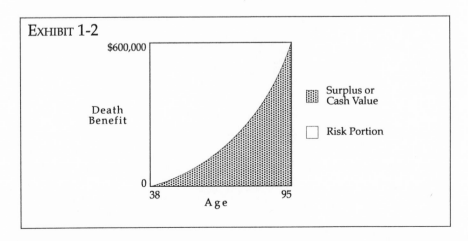

amount of death benefit that is actually being purchased within the policy is $95,000 ($100,000 - $5,000). In a sense the insured is self-insuring $5,000 of the total $100,000 death benefit in the form of the policy's surplus. The policy's surplus has two functions: It reduces the amount of the policy's actual risk portion and it provides funding as the risk portion's unit cost (per $1,000 of risk) increases as the insured grows older.

If the permanent insurance policy is canceled, the policyowner is entitled to the cash value created by the surplus. And depending on the type of permanent insurance policy, the cash value may be borrowed (you pay a specified amount of interest on the amount borrowed) or portions of the cash value may be withdrawn.

I have frequently been asked by clients whether I believe in permanent or term life insurance. Recommending the most appropriate type of life insurance is not a matter of belief. There is nothing spiritual about it. It depends on many factors discussed throughout this book.

I don't begin with a preference for term or permanent life insurance. One is not better than the other. Each basic type of life insurance has an appropriate role. Recommending one over the other depends on individual circumstances.

CHAPTER TWO

THE LIFE INSURANCE FIASCO

The first portion of this book is a life insurance insider's challenge to the commission-motivated system for the marketing and selling of life insurance. This system works well for the life insurance industry and its agents, but it leaves many life insurance consumers confused, frustrated and angry. This chapter exposes the most serious problems associated with the commission-motivated system for the marketing and selling of life insurance.

My claim that many life insurance consumers are confused, frustrated and angry is based on my many experiences with clients who have had very negative experiences with the commission-based delivery system.

There are three significant problems associated with the commission-motivated system for marketing and selling life insurance that are serious enough to result in the exploitation of life insurance consumers.

The first, and by far the most significant, problem with the commission-motivated system is the commission system itself. Life insurance agents are paid a commission by the insurance company for the sale of its policies. These commissions are generally in the range of 50% to 90% of the first-year premium and 5% to 10% of subsequent premiums for another four to nine years, depending on the particular policy sold. The commission structure is the linchpin of the life insurance industry. Without the offer of such a high financial reward for successfully completing the sale of a life insurance policy, the industry would have a very difficult time recruiting agents and convincing them to perform the very distasteful tasks of solicitation and the hard selling of potential buyers.

It is important to understand that commission-motivated selling is not inherently negative. It is only negative when the commission motivation is combined with a wide gap in knowledge between the seller and buyer, and when laws that are intended to regulate this relationship are inadequate, ignored or both. When these conditions are present, there is the strong potential for the seller to be manipulative and distort the message in an attempt to sell products, simply because the prospective buyer has so little knowledge of the product he is considering.

This concept can be appreciated by comparing a recent experience I had purchasing several suits. The salesman, who I assume earns most of his compensation from commissions on the sales he makes, initially attempted to interest me in suits that did not appeal to me. When I ignored these attempts, he stood aside and allowed me to select suits that were to my tastes. Our relationship was not burdened with a gap in knowledge. I knew far better than the salesman what I wanted to purchase and, even though he was commission motivated, he was very helpful after I had selected my suits. This is far different from commission-motivated commercial relationships in which the buyer, because of a lack of knowledge, is at the mercy of the seller.

Professionals with far more knowledge than their clients and patients should not have a financial stake, other than for the services they perform, in the recommendations they make. A surgeon recommending a procedure for a patient, an attorney recommending the drafting of complicated legal documents, and a fee-for-service life insurance adviser recommending the review of a client's existing life insurance policies all have a slight conflict of interest because they are paid for the services they recommend. But these conflicts are minuscule when compared to the conflicts that exist when salesmen, with far superior knowledge compared to their customers, act as advisers for the purchase of products they earn tremendous commissions selling.

Imagine for example, if physicians' only compensation came from the prescription drugs they ordered, selling them for commissions that varied depending on the drugs ordered. Their objectivity would be totally compromised, and because patients have so little knowledge compared to physicians, it would produce a system similar to the commission-motivated system for selling life insurance.

At its worst, this commission delivery system produces something like a zero sum game. The agent is paid only if he is successful in convincing a prospect to buy a policy. The higher the premium, the higher the compensation earned by the agent from the insurance company. Some agents select the policy they will sell based on the level of commission they will receive. Most, if not all, of the decisions made by the agent concerning his recommendations are completely unknown to the prospective buyer. Therefore, the commission system, coupled with a wide gap of knowledge between the buyer and seller, produces tremendous incentive and opportunity for the agent to achieve financial gain at the consumer's expense.

Even under the best of circumstances, this commission delivery system for selling life insurance produces inherent and unavoidable conflicts between the knowledgeable life insurance agent and the ignorant potential buyer.

The second problem with life insurance marketing and selling that is commission motivated is that many consumers don't plan to buy it. This may seem like a rather ridiculous claim until you consider that most consumers are highly resistant to uninvited solicitations, especially to uninvited solicitations concerning the subject of life insurance. This has resulted in highly motivated life insurance agents camouflaging the purpose of their uninvited solicitations. Consumers are frequently sought out by life insurance agents for reasons having little to do with buying life insurance. For example, many life insurance agents have wrapped themselves in the presumed professional aura of financial planner. They solicit potential buyers of life insurance for such things as income tax reduction or increasing investment results, only to turn the engagement into the sale of a life insurance policy. Therefore, there can be very little rational thought given to the purchase of life insurance when it is done during the frenzied embrace of an eager salesman who may have distorted his stated purpose for seeking an appointment in the first place. Michael Lewis, in his excellent book about the investment banking business, *Liar's Poker*, contends that the most dreadful thing a phone can be used for legally is to call someone you don't know and convince them to buy something they don't want. This statement could also apply to life insurance solicitation, with the additional problem of stealth.

If consumers aren't convinced at the time they buy the life insurance policy that there is a compelling reason and rational basis for its purchase, there will be little motivation to continue it when the agent is no longer present to pressure the consumer as each subsequent annual premium comes due. As described in the Introduction, industry studies indicate that nearly half of permanent life insurance policies are canceled within seven years. (See Appendix A. If you are interested in reading about my experiences with agent solicitation distortions and consumer confusion, do so now and then return to this chapter.)

The final serious problem with the commission-motivated system for selling life insurance is that consumers simply don't understand the product they are being pressured to buy. Consumer confusion about life insurance is due to three contributing factors.

The first factor is that there is a myriad of different types of term and permanent life insurance policies, each with its own terminology. This factor in and of itself presents problems because there is no common ground for comparing these different policy designs. And while I don't believe that most insurance companies design their policies to be unnecessarily complex, they also don't go out of their way to design them to be easier to understand, either.

Second, consumer confusion is also due to the life insurance agent's reward system. As described earlier, agents are rewarded (compensated via commissions) for selling a policy, not for providing information intended to inform consumers. Rather, many agents provide life insurance policy information for the sole purpose of convincing the customer to buy the policy that is being recommended. This leads to consumers who do not make their buying decision on the basis of the best comparative information available, but on selective information tightly controlled by the agent.

This problem is compounded because most life insurance purchase decisions are made based on non-guaranteed policy value projections. Too many agents fail to adequately explain the potential consequences of these non-guaranteed factors for fear their customer won't buy the policy. Buying a life insurance policy whose projected values aren't guaranteed, from agents who are compensated only if they can sell it, can be like roller skating on marbles.

The final factor contributing to consumer confusion is the absence of life insurance regulations compelling insurance companies to disclose useful information in a form that can be understood by most consumers. Further, there should be regulations prohibiting the display of information that can be easily misinterpreted by many consumers. At the very least, insurance companies should be required to disclose:

1. The level of agent commissions (including bonus commission arrangements such as expense reimbursement allowances), the level of general agent commissions, and the level of home office marketing allowances, which are credited based on the amount of premium earned for the first and subsequent years. This would inform consumers of the full amount of the policy sales charges and allow them to compare the sales charges for different policies;

2. The assumed and guaranteed cost of insurance rates for

both term and permanent insurance policies. Further, information should be provided about whether the assumed cost of insurance rates are consistent with industry experience or whether they assume improved mortality experience in the future;

3. The investment portfolio used for the investment of the consumers' premiums and a comparison of this portfolio to the industry average; and

4. Pertinent information that could have an impact on a policy's future performance.

The combination of these factors - insurance companies providing policy information that is complex, the rewarding of agents for controlling the information to their advantage, and the absence of life insurance regulations compelling the disclosure of useful information and prohibiting information that is easily misinterpreted - results in consumer confusion over the products they are asked to purchase. (See Appendix B. If you are interested in reading about consumer confusion in purchasing life insurance, do so now and then return to this chapter.)

These three serious problems associated with the commission-motivated system for selling life insurance - the commission reward itself, consumers not intending to buy it, and consumers not understanding life insurance - combine to produce a system that many times leads to consumer exploitation. It is important to note that these serious problems are an integral part of the commission-motivated system for selling life insurance. They are systemic.

There are many organizations and institutions with significant systemic problems that cause difficulties even though many of the individuals within these organizations and institutions are dedicated and well meaning. The current rules allowing our elected national representatives and senators to earn outside income, regulations covering campaign financing and, especially, unlimited terms of office have led many critics to conclude that the national political agenda is suffering. These, it is claimed, are systemic problems that have an adverse effect on the honorable and not so honorable alike.

The systemic nature of the problems with the commission-motivated delivery system for selling life insurance is the reason I do not treat the commission delivery system in a more benign fashion. This commission-motivated delivery system has such serious systemic problems for life insurance agents that both the honorable and dishonorable alike are affected.

While there are some agents who take full advantage of the current system, many agents are decent salesmen trapped in an undesirable system.

Life insurance agents can be classified into three categories. Agents in the first category are, in a narrow sense, like Machiavelli's fox. They know full well what they are doing and will always maximize their advantage, frequently at the expense of their customers. These foxes have perfected the zero sum game in which there is a winner and a loser in their commercial relationship with consumers. It is my sense that these agents are a minority of the life insurance agent force. And I am certain that their fellow agents are as dismayed with their behavior as I am. But they definitely exist, and they can't be identified by any particular personality trait. Consumers without sufficient knowledge to defend themselves from these foxes will continue to be their victims.

Agents in the second category have a better sense of integrity than that exhibited by the foxes, but have been so thoroughly inculcated into the philosophy of the life insurance industry that they are unable to focus on solutions that do not include the purchase of life insurance. Many life insurance agents simply don't have the ability or motivation to question the gospel as established by the life insurance industry because it is in their self-interest to believe industry propaganda. This results in a frantic full court press to sell life insurance as the solution to nearly every problem that can be imagined. Their selling of life insurance is not done with any recognized sense of financial gain at the consumer's expense, as is the case with the fox category, but the results are nearly the same. (See Appendix C. If you are interested in reading about the indoctrination of agents, do so now and then return to this chapter.)

Agents in the final category have a developed sense of integrity with a broader vision than the previous group. However, because of the commission compensation system, they are frequently unable to apply their heightened sense of integrity and fair play. An agent with the best of personal characteristics would still have a difficult time recommending that a prospective life insurance buyer purchase association group term life insurance, which would pay him absolutely no commission, even if such a purchase were decidedly in the consumer's best interest. Even the most responsible agent has to earn a living.

Perhaps an example will offer a vivid portrayal of the inherent problems associated with the commission-motivated system for the marketing and selling of life insurance. The agent in this example is definitely a fox type of agent who took advantage of his clients using the stealth method of solicitation and presenting information that was misinterpreted by the clients in order to complete his mission at the substantial expense of his clients.

Several years ago I was retained by a large law firm in the Detroit area, as a fee-for-service life insurance adviser, to review life insurance policies they had purchased the year before. The previous year, the law firm had been contacted by a representative of a local brokerage firm. This representative identified himself as a financial consultant who proposed that he would objectively review their qualified retirement plan. In claiming his objectivity, he favorably contrasted himself to life insurance agents who are, after all, known to lack objectivity.

The 'financial consultant' discovered that the life insurance policies purchased for the law partners in their qualified retirement plan were a poor choice and recommended that they be canceled and replaced with policies sold by a Michigan based life insurance company, which he claimed were a much better value. (Both the existing and proposed new policies were permanent forms of life insurance.) The partners of this law firm were impressed by the significantly higher projected accumulation value that was demonstrated in the proposal illustrations for the recommended replacement policies. (Proposal illustrations are ledgers showing the projected cash values and death benefits of a particular policy, based on guaranteed and non-guaranteed pricing factors). Based on the proposal illustrations the law partners accepted the recommendation made by this 'financial consultant' and replaced their existing policies with the recommended replacement policies.

The law partners became suspicious when, as required by law, the local brokerage firm representative had to disclose his commission compensation from the sale of these life insurance policies at the end of the fiscal year since they were sold to a qualified retirement plan. The combined annual premiums for the recommended replacement policies totaled approximately $25,000. The disclosed commission compensation was $22,500. This represents a commission rate of 90%.

It should be noted that this commission disclosure requirement is not mandated by any of the various regulations concerning the sale of life insurance. It is required by federal laws regulating qualified retirement plans. This commission disclosure requirement is needed for certain forms relating to the qualified retirement plan only at the end of the fiscal year, not before the purchase of the life insurance when the disclosure of the commission rate would have some relevance to the purchase decision.

The day after learning the amount of the commission earned by the 'financial consultant,' the law firm hired me to review the purchase of the recommended replacement policies. Since all of the partners had purchased the identical policy, I reviewed the senior partner's policy as representative of the entire purchase.

I discovered that this 'financial consultant' had sold the law partners the highest commission-paying policy offered by the

Michigan based life insurance company - a policy called the Ultimate I. This policy pays a 90% first-year commission. Unknown to the partners was that this company also offered a policy called the Preferred Ultimate I, which has a commission rate of 45%. The major non-economic difference between the two policies is that, while they both have non-smoker rates and are both sold to non-smokers, the Preferred Ultimate I isn't available to smokers.

Exhibit 2-1 is a chart distributed by the Michigan based company to life insurance agents describing the features of their various cash value policies. Interestingly, the category at the top of the page is the agent's commission rate. This chart was

Exhibit 2-1

Features	Ultimate I	Preferred Ultimate I	Ultimate II	Preferred Ultimate II	Ultimate V	Ultimate Plus	"Group" Ultimate Plus	Joint Ultimate	Last Survivor	Enhanced Ultimate	HiLife
Comission 1st year / 2-10 / 11-on	90% / 7.5% / 1%	45% / 5% / 1%	80% / 5% / 1%	70% / 5% / 1%	80% / 5% / 1%	80% / 5% / 1%	60% 25%-Yr. 2 / 5%-Yrs.3-10 / 1% - 11-on	80% / 5% / 1%	80% / 5% / 1%	60% / 3.5% / 1%	80% / 5% / 1%
Current Interest Rate											
Face Guarantee	Life	Life	Life	Life	Life	Life	Life	Life	Life	Life	Life
Rate/$1,000 guarantee	10 years	10 years	Life	Life	Life	10 years	10 years	Life	10 years	Life	Life
Vanish Premium	No	Yes	Yes	Yes	Yes	Yes	Yes	Yes	Yes	Yes	Yes
Non-smoker Rates	Yes	Yes	Yes	Yes	Yes	No	No	No	Yes	Yes	Yes
Underwritten Substandard	Yes	No	Yes	No	Yes	Yes	Yes	Yes	Yes	Yes	Yes
Minimum Face Amount	$50,000	$100,000	$10,000	$100,000	$50,000	$10,000	$5,000	$25,000	$100,000	$50,000	$50,000
Age Written (Last Birthday) Minimum / Maximum	25 / 80	35 / 80	0-80 Standard / 20-80 Non-smoker	20 / 80	20 / 80	0 / 80	20 / 65	20 / 65	35 / 75	0-80 Standard / 20-80 Non-smoker	0-80 Standard / 20-80 Non-smoker
Available for Conversion To	Yes	No	Yes	No	Yes	Yes	No	Yes	No	Yes	Yes
Conversion Credits	None	N/A	None	N/A	None	Last gross annual premium	N/A	None	N/A	None	None

obviously not intended for public consumption.

The 45% commission policy, the Preferred Ultimate I, requires lower premiums and has a higher cash value than the 90% commission policy (Ultimate I). Exhibit 2-2 compares the annual premium, accumulation account, and projected surrender value of the 90% commission policy (Ultimate I) with the 45% commission policy (Preferred Ultimate I). Remember that the law firm partners were sold the 90% commission policy (Ultimate I). Exhibit 2-2 is a recap of proposal illustrations for each policy for the senior partner of the law firm:

EXHIBIT 2-2

INSURANCE AMOUNT: $500,000
50 YEAR-OLD MALE NON-SMOKER

	Ultimate I 90% Comission Policy Annual Premium - $6,830		Preferred Ultimate I 45% Commission Policy Annual Premium - $6,400	
Policy Year	Accumulation Account	Surrender Value	Accumulation Account	Surrender Value
1	$5,270	0	$5,770	0
2	10,820	2,315	11,980	4,015
3	16,685	8,180	18,695	10,725
4	22,870	14,365	25,945	17,975
5	29,370	20,860	33,765	25,795
10	66,165	59,360	82,465	76,090
15	111,320	107,920	152,775	149,590
20	167,145	167,145	257,790	257,790
30	351,850	351,850	696,080	696,080

By selling the highest commission policy offered by the Michigan based company the financial consultant increased his commission compensation by over $11,000 for the combined sale of the Ultimate I (90% commission) policies to all the law partners, compared to the commission that would have been earned had he sold the Preferred Ultimate I policy (45% commission), or another companies' policy with a substantially lower commission rate.

It's a pretty good trick when you can sell a policy with a higher premium and offer a significantly lower policy surrender value.

The partners made the decision to cancel their existing life insurance and buy the Ultimate I policies based on the accumu-lation account column from the proposal illustrations presented by the 'financial consultant.' Unfortunately, the accumulation account is a fiction! The accumulation account can't be borrowed against, it can't be used to pay premiums, nor does it represent the value of the policy if it is canceled. In other words, the accumulation account only exists as ink on the proposal illustration and annual policy statements. The partners were either intentionally misled by the 'financial consultant,' or he passively allowed the partners to assume that the accumulation account actually existed. The only column that is meaningful is the surrender value column. The accumulation account columns are included in Exhibit 2-2 to demonstrate how confusing this life insurance proposal illustration is. Liar's poker, anyone?

In fact, the senior partner was still under the impression that the accumulation account was the value of his policy when I was hired to review their policies. This mistaken impression was reinforced by the annual policy statement, which is sent to policyholders. Exhibit 2-3, on page 19, is the first annual policy statement received by the senior partner.

The highlighted portion of this annual policy statement indicates the policy's accumulation account. Note that the only mention of the surrender charges is at the bottom of the statement. I particularly find the statement "In the absence of surrender, your next year's accumulation account will increase by $5,666.76 to $11,033.79," to be a significant distortion. As stated earlier, the accumulation account is a total fiction. The only value this policy has is it's surrender value, which after the first year is zero. The fact that a highly educated senior partner of a large law firm could confuse the difference between the accumulation account and the surrender value is good evidence that the life insurance industry and its agents can take advantage of unsuspecting consumers.

Exhibit 2-4, on page 20, illustrates these policies without the fictitious accumulation account columns. It displays only the

Exhibit 2-3

```
                                              FEBRUARY 23, 1987
OWNER                       POLICY NO.       :
INSURED                     PLAN             : ULTIMATE I-85
                                               (NON SMOKER)
                            POLICY DATE      : APRIL 23, 1986
TROY, MI   48098            DEATH BENEFIT    : $500,000.00
                            BASE ANNUAL PREMIUM : $6,830.00
                            (EXCLUDING ANY SUPPLEMENTAL BENEFIT
DEAR POLICYHOLDER,          PREMIUMS AS INDICATED IN YOUR POLICY)
```

THIS ULTIMATE POLICY PROVIDES LIFE INSURANCE PROTECTION AT VERY COMPETETIVE RATES PLUS OUTSTANDING, TAX-SHELTERED CASH ACCUMULATION BASED ON AN INTEREST RATE REFLECTING CURRENT ECONOMIC CONDITIONS. THE CURRENT AND PROJECTED STATUS OF YOUR POLICY IS SHOWN BELOW.

	PAST YEAR*	NEXT YEAR**
CURRENT INTEREST RATE	11.20%	9.20%
VALUE ACCUMULATION ACCOUNT AT 4/23/1986	$.00	
AMOUNTS ADDED TO ACCOUNT		
FROM PREMIUM	$6,830.00	$6,830.00
AMOUNTS DEDUCTED FROM ACCOUNT		
COST OF DEATH BENEFIT INCLUDING POLICY FEE	$2,003.53	$2,191.12
VALUE OF ACCUMULATION ACCOUNT AS OF		
4/23/1987 AND 4/23/1988	**$5,367.03**	**$11,033.79**
TOTAL NET INCREASE FROM 4/23/1986 TO		
4/23/1987 AND FROM 4/23/1987 TO 4/23/1988	$5,367.03	$5,666.76

*VALUES FOR THE PAST YEAR ARE BASED ON PREMIUM PAYMENTS TO THE CURRENT POLICY
 DATE. VALUES FOR THE NEXT YEAR ASSUME THE POLICY IS NOT SURRENDERED OR
 BORROWED AGAINST DURING THE NEXTPOLICY YEAR AND PREMIUMS ARE PAID AS DUE.
*VALUES FOR THE NEXT YEAR ARE BASED ON AN 11.20% RATE ON PREVIOUS PREMIUMS AND
 A 9.20% RATE ON NEW PREMIUMS AND REDEPOSITED INTEREST.

FOR THE UPCOMING POLICY YEAR, YOUR DEATH BENEFIT WILL BE $500,000.00.
IN THE EVENT YOUR POLICY IS SURRENDERED DURING THE NEXT YEAR, **YOUR CASH VALUE
WILL BE THE AMOUNT OF YOUR ACCUMULATION ACCOUNT LESS THE SURRENDER CHARGE OF
$8,506.25.** THIS CHARGE DECREASES EACH YEAR AS A PERCENT OF THE ACCUMULATION
ACCOUNT UNTIL IT DISAPPEARS. **IN THE ABSENCE OF SURRENDER, YOUR NEXT YEAR'S
ACCUMULATION ACCOUNT WILL INCREASE BY $5,666,76 TO $11,033.79.**
PLEASE DIRECT ANY INQUIRES TO LIFE POLICYHOLDERS SERVICE.

EXHIBIT 2-4

INSURANCE AMOUNT: $500,000
50 YEAR-OLD MALE NON-SMOKER

Policy Year	Ultimate I 90% Comission Policy Annual Premium - $6,830 Cash Value	Preferred Ultimate I 45% Commission Policy Annual Premium - $6,400 Cash Value
1	0	0
2	2,315	4,015
3	8,180	10,725
4	14,365	17,975
5	20,860	25,795
10	59,360	76,090
15	107,920	149,590
20	167,145	257,790
30	351,850	696,080

surrender value columns, which should be referred to as the policy cash value. The actual cash value is the only policy value information that should be presented to consumers.

This case combines the problems I have identified with the marketing and selling of life insurance. The local brokerage firm representative motivated by the high commissions he could earn, misled the partners of this law firm about his real intentions by claiming to be a financial consultant who would review their qualified retirement plan. He then used the safety of proposal illustrations that can be easily misinterpreted to convince them to replace their existing policies with policies that were a very poor choice. This life insurance agent gained a tremendous financial advantage at the law partners' expense.

The problems associated with the commission-motivated system have produced an ethical dilemma for the life insurance industry. This has prompted some insurance companies to offer tapes and classes on agent ethics. Unfortunately, these tapes and classes won't have much of an effect on agent behavior as long as the nature of their compensation remains the same. Robin Derry, ethics professor for the American College in Bryn Mawr, Penn., was quoted in the February 18, 1991, issue of Financial Services Week as saying, "Many companies actually undermine their own efforts to cultivate a more ethical sales force. They do that by maintaining, among other things, compensation systems, management structures and product choices that make it difficult for agents to be ethical out in the field." Dr. Derry went on to say, "You can change behavior by the way you pay people."

CHAPTER THREE

LIFE INSURANCE AND FINANCIAL PLANNERS

There is an increasing number of life insurance agents selling investment products and an increasing number of investment product salesmen who are now selling life insurance. Both groups are increasingly identifying themselves as financial planners. This chapter examines the practice of life insurance agents identifying themselves as financial planners and offers a brief critique of personal financial planning in general. This critique isn't necessarily important to my life insurance topic, but may be a preview of a later book.

Personal financial planning is an infant profession struggling for an identity. Some life insurance and investment salesmen, in trying to upgrade their image, have been wrapping themselves in the presumed professional garments of financial planning. In reality, these insurance and investment salesmen are using this presumed positive image as camouflage to sell their products and earn their commissions. According to a 1989 survey conducted by the International Association of Financial Planners, 79% of its members earn some or all of their compensation from commissions. This figure is nearly identical to the 80% of certified financial planners (CFPs) who earn some or all of their compensation from commissions, according to the most recent survey of CFPs in 1987.

In Chapter Two, I stated that one of the three serious problems with buying life insurance under the commission-motivated system is that many buyers of life insurance didn't intend to buy it. This situation occurs because life insurance agents usually don't solicit a potential customer for the stated purpose of selling them life insurance. A frequent solicitation method of life insurance agents is the offer to provide the prospective customer with comprehensive financial planning. Offers of estate planning, tax-deferred investments, etc., are made in order to interest the prospect in meeting the solicitor.

Only after a rather time-consuming process of collecting financial data and presenting reports does the unsuspecting consumer realize that the whole point to this engagement is the sale of life insurance. The reason most consumers financial problems are solved by the purchase of life insurance is because of the commission level for the sale of life insurance, which is far greater than the commission level for the sale of investment products. Remember that life insurance commissions are in the range of 50% to 90% of the first-year premium, whereas commissions for load mutual funds are generally 4% to 8%.

This transparent fiction of pretending to provide objective personal financial planning when the real goal is to sell life insurance for the commissions they pay is increasingly alienating consumers to the entire financial planning profession. And there is a good deal of conflict within the financial planning profession, in large part because they haven't figured out how to elevate their previous status as salesmen to one of professional financial planner without giving up the very lucrative commission compensation.

According to an article appearing in the February 4, 1991, issue of *Financial Services Week* written by Gregory Bresiger, the International Board of Standards and Practices for Certified Financial Planners (IBCFP) had drafted proposed professional practice standards. According to Mr. Bresiger, the draft proposals contain two particularly controversial standards. One would be a requirement that CFPs "...disclose the estimated amount of total compensation, including fees and commissions." This, Mr. Bresiger writes, "...is sure to be a sore point with some planners, who believe the requirement would put them at a competitive disadvantage with other financial service professionals." Another standard, "... would require CFPs to owe their first loyalty to the client as a fiduciary, a high standard that some in the industry believe could more easily open up planners to lawsuits."

In June 1991 the IBCFP decided not to take a vote on these two controversial standards. What they discovered was that salesmen and fee-for-service advisers' motivations are so different that it wasn't possible to reach a consensus on them.

Richard Schickel, a movie critic for *Time Magazine*, could have been describing the current state of affairs within much of the financial planning profession, when he stated that his book, *Intimate Strangers* is about "...the battle for the soul of a culture seduced and battered by machinery that puts image before substance and claims before creativity."

One of the major tools of financial planning is the computer, with the appropriate selection of software programs that are suited for particular purposes. In general, there are three varieties of software programs. If you can understand the software's purpose, you can figure out what the financial planner is up to.

The first variety is used by commission-motivated investment and life insurance salesmen. These programs are solutions looking for problems. The data is computed in a manner to justify recommendations for the purchase of investment and insurance products the salesmen have available.

The computer allows investment and life insurance salesmen without the necessary experience or knowledge to identify themselves as financial planners. It's something like the old saying, "Last week I couldn't even spell engineer and now I are one." All they really need to know is how to solicit a prospective buyer and fill out a financial data form. This data is entered into the computer and the 'financial plan' magically appears with recommendations to buy certain investment and insurance products. When a computer tells you to invest in a high-yielding bond fund and to purchase permanent life insurance, how can you argue with such high-tech objectivity?

An experience I had as a brokerage manager for an insurance agency highlights the tactic of abruptly changing life insurance agents into financial planners with the aid of financial planning software.

The recruiting and training manager for this life insurance agency recruited potential agents with a help-wanted ad for financial planners. On at least two occasions while in this manager's office, I heard him deny to callers that the advertised position was for selling life insurance. He was distorting the position for which recruits were being hired. Once hired, the recruits were given a week (or two weeks) training course. One woman hired as a 'financial planner,' suddenly realized on Thursday of the training week that the primary purpose of her new job was to sell life insurance. Upon this discovery, she gathered her things and left, never to be heard from again.

With such a limited amount of training time, these recruits were primarily taught how to solicit, give an introductory pitch to prospective customers and fill out the financial data form that would be input into the computer. Once 'trained,' these 'financial planners' were given a mailing list from which they sent out letters identifying their organization as the foremost financial planning firm in Michigan. This claim was rather audacious when you consider that the life insurance agency had only several months before decided to identify its agents as financial planners.

Unfortunately, these recruits had no sense of what they were doing. I recall being asked to sit in on a practice session with a newly hired financial planner preparing for a customer presentation. The customers had a combined annual income of $60,000. The computer, searching for the largest life insurance sale it could justify, had projected the value of this couple's assets far into the future and then noted an estate tax problem many years away. The solution for this electronically imagined estate tax problem was for the couple to buy life insurance now to fund this projected future problem. The annual premium for the recommended life insurance purchase was $6,000. Anybody with any sense would realize that buying life insurance with an annual premium equal to 10% of your gross income (remember this couple's gross annual income was $60,000) is ridiculous.

What makes this example extraordinary is the distortion used in hiring life insurance agents in the first place. I suppose the lesson is that the life insurance industry not only has a difficult time in soliciting consumers to listen to their appeals to buy life insurance, but they also have a difficult time hiring agents to do this work.

The second variety of financial planning software programs provides generic, non-specific financial planning information. The information presented has no relevance to any specific client and it isn't used to sell investment or insurance products. These programs are primarily used by medium-sized CPA (certified public accountant) firms.

A few CPA firms have fallen into the belief that they must provide their clients with financial planning, even though they don't have anyone on staff who has much knowledge or experience with financial planning. They have purchased these generic financial planning software programs as a way of providing financial planning services, without really knowing much about them. The approach hasn't met with much success.

Several years ago I received a solicitation letter from a software company offering a financial planning software package. The letter began:

"Dear Professional:

Imagine pressing one key on your computer and printing out a comprehensive, CUSTOMIZED report, up to 50 pages long, for each of the clients for whom you do financial planning."

Imagine indeed! This has led one critic of financial planning to refer to such generic financial planning software as 'Plan Man.'

The final variety of financial planning software programs is a good deal more sophisticated and is used primarily by fee-only financial planning firms and large CPA firms. These programs aren't designed to be selling tools for investment and insurance products and they are specific to the needs of individual financial planning clients.

However, these sophisticated financial planning software programs encourage the primacy of overly precise and frequently redundant financial calculations instead of understanding the client's motivations and desires. The amount of statistical information given simply overwhelms the client. This makes it very difficult for the planner and client to focus on those few areas of particular significance that need attention and action.

Imagine going to your physician for a physical exam and being presented with a 100-page, leather-bound report detailing the precise calculations and irrelevant descriptions of the blood analysis, EKG, scopes and scans, plus a projection of your health status in 10 years. The only point to such a report would be to charge a much larger fee for the physical exam. And that is exactly the major motivation for the 100-page, leather bound financial plan.

This motivation is my major objection to sophisticated computer-generated financial plans: That they provide the justification for charging fees that are entirely too high. If the charge for such plans had some relationship to the time it took to input the data and analyze the results, they really wouldn't be offensive, just not very useful. Their uselessness is especially apparent if you consider that massaging the financial data to provide projections is completely dependent on three factors remaining constant: the tax law, the economic environment, and the client's goals or financial situation - factors that are constantly changing.

An attorney acquaintance of mine told of a recent experience he had working with a national CPA firm. The attorney and the national CPA firm shared a common client. The CPA firm had produced one of these 100-page, leather bound financial plan specials at a cost of $8,000, with no specific investment recommendations made. One month after the delivery of the financial plan, the client sold his closely-held business, which was by far his largest asset. This sale caused the financial plan, which had initially been superfluous, to become completely worthless. The CPA firm offered to remassage the numbers for the discount rate of $5,000. This offer was wisely rejected.

These problems associated with personal financial planning may be worked out over time as the profession matures and is regulated by market forces. Many in the financial planning profession may not have very good sense, but consumers will simply not respond to financial planning that is the transparent justification for selling commission-paying insurance and investment products, done by their local CPA without the requisite experience, nor will they agree to pay enormous fees for financial data massaging. The national CPA firm described above has sold off its financial services subsidiary. I assume that this was done because too many of this CPA firm's clients felt that their financial planning was being done to them instead of for them. Way to go, consumers!

If personal financial planning is to become a true profession, its practitioners must learn how to deal with clients in a simpler and more direct fashion, and they must be compensated directly by the client based on the advisory services provided. Further, financial planners must recognize their limitations and refer their clients to other professionals with special skills in specific areas, such as sophisticated life insurance planning or qualified retirement plan design. Finally, financial planners not only must have the ability to make a diagnosis, but they must also be able to provide their clients with a prescription. I envision a financial planning profession that operates in a fashion similar to the medical profession, where general practitioners and internists are paid for their services, not by commissions earned for procedures recommended, and refer their clients to specialists when it is appropriate.

Chapter Four

The Rebate Debate and the Influence of the Life Insurance Industry

The issues raised in this chapter are not mentioned for their current news value (some of them may have temporary or permanent resolutions by the time this book is published), but as examples of the influence the life insurance industry has on state governments and their life insurance regulators. Such influence, I'm afraid, will be a timeless problem. Paul A. Gigot referred to this type of problem in his March 8, 1991, *Wall Street Journal* column, "Potomac Watch." He wrote, "With communism dead... Freedom's main enemy now is the corporate state, private business harnessed to the coercive power of government."

The term rebate, as it applies to life insurance, refers to the return of some or all of the commissions earned from the sale of a life insurance policy to the purchaser of that policy. If you are using this book as a guide for your personal life insurance planning and purchases, the rebating issue is of little importance because no-commission policies (described later) are generally a much better buy for you, anyway.

No-commission term and no-commission universal life policies are the most appropriate recommendation for 90% or more of fee-for-service life insurance advisers' clients. However, there are several types of life insurance policies that might be appropriate under certain circumstances that aren't currently available on a no-commission basis, or aren't available from companies I would recommend.

When a commission-paying policy is deemed the most appropriate purchase, a fee-for-service life insurance adviser might consider rebating all commissions paid by the insurance company to the client in exchange for his hourly fees.

Unfortunately, every state except Florida and California considers commission rebates illegal. Florida's anti-rebate statute was ruled unconstitutional in 1986 when its Supreme Court upheld the First District Court of Appeals and California's anti-rebate statute was eliminated by Proposition 103 in 1988.

In November of 1987, I filed suit against the Michigan insurance commissioner, claiming that the anti-rebate laws are not permitted by the Michigan constitution. In essence, my claim is that anti-rebate laws protect life insurance agents, not consumers, from new forms of competition, and therefore they violate the due process clause of the Michigan constitution. I asked for the right to rebate 100% of any commissions I may earn to the client in exchange for my hourly fees. Rebating and recommending policies that pay the adviser no commissions are the only ways to remove the tremendous conflict of interest inherent in the commission system of life insurance selling.

While this legal action is largely symbolic since over 90% of my clients are better served by a no-commission policy, all consumers would benefit by a victory in this case.

In July 1990 Ingham County Circuit Court ruled that any change in the anti-rebate laws should be taken up with the Michigan legislature and ruled against my contention that anti-rebate laws are unconstitutional. Judge Glazer wrote for the court, "In other words, the Plaintiff must show that the legislative judgment is utterly without rational foundation." This is a very stringent test for me to meet.

In contrast to Judge Glazer's stringent test, the test imposed by the First District Court of Appeals in Florida was much less severe. That court ruled 5-0 that the anti-rebate statutes were unconstitutional, a decision upheld by the Florida Supreme Court in June of 1986. In part, their decision stated, "We are unable to find any legitimate state interest justifying the continued existence of the anti-rebate statutes...In the absence of any apparent rational relation between the prohibition of rebates and some legitimate state purpose in safeguarding the public welfare, we conclude the anti-rebate statutes...constitute an unjustified exercise of the police power of this state..."

I am appealing my trial court ruling and I am hopeful the Michigan Court of Appeals will apply the less stringent test.

I recognize that reasonable men and women can disagree on whether the courts should impose the "utterly without rational foundation" or the "rational relationship" test in judging the statutes regulating business relations enacted by state legislatures. Supporting one side or the other does not necessarily center on the issue of judicial activism, but rather the importance the court gives to each side's explanation of the predictable consequences of freeing the life insurance industry from price fixing.

Regardless of the outcome of this case, the problems facing life insurance consumers are not being adequately addressed because state governments and their regulators are substantially influenced by the life insurance industry.

This influence may explain a Michigan statute that establishes penalties for consumers who receive commission rebates. This statute provides that a consumer accepting an illegal rebate must forfeit death benefits based on the percentage of rebate received to the total premium. Can you imagine a grieving widow being informed that, because her husband received a rebate of 50% of the premium, the state was forcing the insurance company to withhold 50% of the death benefit?

It may also explain Michigan statutes regulating a special license (Life Insurance Counselors - LIC) that provides for counselors charging a fee for their services. The various statutes regulating the LIC license provide that a counselor may also accept commissions from the sale of life insurance policies, in addition to the fees charged. However, there is a specific statute making it illegal to reduce a counselor's fee by the amount of commission he may earn from selling a policy. In other words, the state demands that a counselor, also acting as an agent, must be paid twice - directly from fees paid by the client and from commissions paid by the insurance company.

The needs and arguments of the life insurance industry and agent associations, in my judgment, are simply too invasive into the legal, administrative and legislative processes. My particular challenge to the anti-rebate statute was joined by the Independent Insurance Agents of Michigan, Michigan State Association of Life Underwriters and Michigan Association of Professional Insurance Agents. Numerous reports and briefs were filed from national groups and life insurance companies as well. The industry's briefs in my case were at least 90% of the paper filed for the other side. In the trial court's decision, Judge Glazer quoted liberally from a 'study' prepared and paid for by Prudential Insurance Company of America. Judge Glazer referred to this material as "typical of materials submitted by Defendants." On the other hand, Judge Glazer referred to as typical for our side the testimony of Wisconsin Insurance Commissioner Susan Mitchell before the Sub-Committee on General Oversight of the House of Representatives Committee on Small Business, September 21, 1981.

Judge Glazer may not even realize that he chose to recite as typical for the Defendants a brief written on behalf of the largest life insurance company in America. Whereas, he recited as typical for my side the words of a very courageous state insurance commissioner before a U.S. Congressional committee hearing.

Generally, the life insurance industry's influence over issues it believes are important are established on an *a priori* basis. However, they have had to play catch-up to exert their influence on legal rebating. Three specific instances come to mind. First, since 1987 I have been advertising the availability of wholesale costs for life insurance purchases for consumers either by selling no-commission policies or by selling a full-commission policy in Florida, where it is legal to rebate, and rebating the full commission in exchange for my hourly fee. On four separate occasions the

Michigan Insurance Bureau approved this advertising and offer, and in fact they submitted an affidavit to this effect with the court in association with my legal action challenging the anti-rebate statute.

In April 1990, a local life insurance agent informed me that Frank Kelly, Michigan's attorney general, told a general agent's group that his office was looking into my advertising and offer to rebate in Florida. Several weeks later I was informed by the same agent that I would be receiving a letter concerning this matter.

So I wasn't surprised when I received a letter from the Michigan Insurance Bureau, dated July 24, 1990, informing me that my advertising and offer was now considered in violation of state statutes. One of the individuals receiving a copy of this letter was an attorney for the various agent groups (Intervenors) opposed to my legal action. Upon further inquiry, I discovered the abrupt reversal concerning my rebate offer when applications are signed in Florida was instigated based on letters of complaint from the attorneys for the Intervenors. In other words, the attorney general and the insurance commissioner reversed their three and a half year approval of my rebate offer based on complaints from my competitors, not from consumers.

This new interpretation of the Michigan insurance statutes that currently prevents agents from offering to rebate commissions in Florida or California was explained in detail in a Declaratory Ruling (91-11498-M) issued in response to my request for a ruling.

The implications of this Declaratory Ruling have significant ramifications for Michigan residents. While it is perfectly legal in Michigan to inform consumers of the availability of commission rebates in Florida and California, and it is legal for a Michigan resident to receive a commission rebate when the insurance application is signed in Florida or California, this ruling makes it illegal for an agent to make a rebate offer to a Michigan resident. Therefore, this ruling may make it impossible for a Michigan resident to receive a commission rebate anywhere.

I am in the process of initiating a challenge to this ruling in Federal District Court. My position will be that this ruling effectively prohibits my exercise of free speech.

Another example of possible behind the scenes industry influence is the reaction of the Florida regulators to legal rebating. After the Florida Supreme Court upheld the First District Court of Appeal's decision that the Florida anti- rebate statute was unconstitutional in 1986, the Florida Department of Insurance claimed that the status of rebating remained unclear because other statutes were not addressed by the court's decision. In a letter to my attorney, dated October 23, 1986, an attorney for this department stated that there were four other statutes that might still prevent rebating. By December of that year the Florida insurance commissioner, Bill Gunter, had settled on one of these other statutes and published a statement that the anti-discrimination provisions of their Insurance Code would be applicable to rebating.

This statute "prohibits discrimination between insureds in the same actuarial class in the rates of premiums charged for life insurance." The statement went on to explain, "In view of these Code provisions it appears that if an agent rebated a given portion of his commission to a particular insured, all insureds in the same actuarial class would have to be afforded the same commission percentage rebate." I am strongly in favor of giving each client the same rebate. In my case the rebate would be 100%. On the surface it would appear that the Florida Department of Insurance is standing foursquare on the side of consumers. However, it is the opinion of agents interested in rebating that the anti-discrimination statute is being used to discourage them from offering any rebates in Florida. The statute would make it illegal to give a consumer buying a policy with little commission a small percentage rebate while giving a consumer buying a policy with a large commission a much larger percentage rebate. For example, a consumer purchasing a policy with a $500 commission might be given a 20% rebate, or $100, while a consumer purchasing a policy with a $5,000 commission might be given an 80% rebate, or $4,000. In the first instance the rebating agent would earn $400 and in the second instance he would earn $1,000. Such an application of the anti-discrimination statute would prevent agents who want to rebate from doing what nearly every other businessman can do - negotiate the price of their product with individual consumers and not be forced to deal with every consumer the same way. Would it be legitimate for state governments to mandate that auto dealers give every customer the same price and rebate for every car they sell, or for appliance stores to give customers the same price and rebate for every refrigerator they sell?

Since the anti-discrimination statute existed long before the anti-rebate statutes were ruled unconstitutional in Florida, the logical inference is that this statute applies to life insurance companies, not agents. So the question is: Has Florida ever enforced this statute against life insurance companies that sell policies, side by side, with different pricing and policy values as in the case of the Ultimate I and Preferred Ultimate I policies (both for sale in Florida) described in Chapter Two? As far as I can determine, this statute has not been enforced against companies that offer policies with different pricing structures like the two policies described in Chapter Two. Why the sudden interest in the anti-discrimination statute that some legal experts claim doesn't even apply to agents? A cynic could speculate that the previously ignored anti-discrimination statute has become a handy tool to discourage a practice the industry is totally against.

Michigan also has an anti-discrimination statute nearly identical to Florida's. And as far as I can determine, Michigan's life insurance regulators have never enforced it against companies offering policies with different pricing structures either.

Another instance of possible life insurance industry influence in the aftermath of legal rebating in Florida is an action the Florida legislature took in August 1990. Not satisfied with relying on the anti-discrimination statute to regulate rebating, they passed a new regulation requiring agents who intend to rebate to publish their rebating scheme with the Florida Department of Insurance and with the insurance companies whose policies they intend to sell. Again, agents interested in rebating believe this regulation will further hamper their ability to rebate. The concern is that insurance companies may refuse to do business with agents who intend to rebate because of pressure from other agents who believe rebating is heresy. This fear is not farfetched. I have had conversations with several excellent companies and I haven't found one that, when informed that an agent will rebate, will do business with that agent. Northwestern Mutual, a stellar company, has made it a contract violation for agents to rebate commissions, even where it is legal.

The good news is that as companies refuse to do business with agents who file their intentions to rebate, these agents may have an excellent anti-trust case.

Regardless of these problems, I am not in favor of giving insurance departments the authority to impose stifling regulations on life insurance transactions or to hire an army of investigators. Rather, what is needed, in addition to the elimination of the anti-rebate laws, is a requirement that full disclosure be given to life insurance consumers, as described in Chapter Two. Mandated disclosure would require political action. This is an issue that needs to be taken up by consumer lobbies because the issues are too complicated, consumer interest is too diffuse and the powerful life insurance industry is opposed to full disclosure. However, I doubt that even consumers lobbies would prevail over the life insurance industry in the political arena. Consumers should demand that any agent trying to sell them life insurance voluntarily disclose the information mentioned in Chapter Two on a form signed by an officer of the company. If the agent won't provide you with this information, find another who will. You can use this information to compare different policies. This advice is for consumers who are not able to follow the life insurance planning and purchase recommendations in this book.

In addition, consumer lobbies should pay more attention to state insurance regulators. Pressure should be exerted when it is perceived that these regulators are interfering with new forms of competition on behalf of the life insurance industry and its agents, rather than regulating the industry on behalf of consumers.

CHAPTER FIVE

HOW TO AVOID THE LIFE INSURANCE FIASCO

While it might be fun to beat up on the life insurance industry and its agents, there really is no point to it unless there are better delivery systems available for astute consumers who wish to avoid the commission-motivated system. This chapter will introduce you to several systems available for your life insurance planning and purchases that can provide you with relief from the exploitation of the commission-motivated system. The remaining chapters provide easy to understand information about determining the amount of life insurance you should own, what kind of life insurance you should buy, and how to buy it at wholesale prices by buying policies with drastically reduced sales charges.

There have been consumer-oriented publications about life insurance that have attempted, as this book does, to inform consumers about life insurance. While many of these publications, in my opinion, have been too complicated for most consumers to understand, excellent information was presented. But until recently, consumers had no outlet to effectively use this information.

Most of these publications concluded by recommending that the reader select a good life insurance agent to work with. It has been my experience that it is very difficult to work with life insurance agents based on a consumer's agenda. Life insurance agents are trained to control the agenda and manipulate the relationship to their advantage.

Whatever the amount of information this book, or any other for that matter, is able to impart, it wouldn't be worth the paper it was printed on if the final word was finding a life insurance agent to assist you. If that were the conclusion of this book, I wouldn't have bothered to write it. Now, however, there are much better options for consumers.

Recent marketing developments provide life insurance consumers with two alternatives to the commission-driven delivery system. They are direct-response and fee-for-service delivery systems.

Both the direct-response and fee-for-service life insurance adviser systems are possible because of two life insurance companies that offer no-commission term and no-commission universal life (a permanent form of insurance) for sale on a direct basis. That is, you can buy your life insurance directly from them at wholesale costs. These life insurance companies are Ameritas Life Insurance Corporation (800/552- 3553) and USAA Life Insurance Company (800/531-8000). Both Ameritas and USAA are rated A+ Superior by A. M. Best, which is Best's highest rating. Ameritas is rated AA (third out of 19 ranking catagories, considered an excellent rating) by Standard & Poor's and A (second out of 16 ranking catagories) by Weiss Research, Inc. In fact, Weiss rates Ameritas as the fifth strongest life insurance company in America. USAA is rated A- (excellent rating) by Weiss Research, Inc.

Presently, Ameritas is not selling low-load policies in New York, New Jersey, Maine or the District of Columbia. USAA is licensed to do business in every state and the District of Columbia. (See Appendix D for information about Ameritas and USAA.)

Ameritas and USAA are the only insurance companies offering low-load, no-commission life insurance policies to consumers on a direct basis. Four other insurance companies offer low- load, no-commission policies on a national basis, but none sell to consumers on a direct basis. Rather, these other four companies require that consumers select a fee-for-service life insurance adviser to explain the policy, and complete and sign the application. While the retention of a fee-for-service life insurance adviser is desirable for a number of situations, it isn't necessary for most life insurance purchases -such a requirement only adds to the cost for consumers.

If other outstanding life insurance companies, such as Northwestern Mutual, designed excellent low-load, no-commission policies and sold them on a direct basis to consumers, I would recommend them with the same enthusiasm I recommend the no- commission policies sold by Ameritas and USAA.

Appendix E has schedules for Ameritas and USAA life insurance rates and instructions on how to compute the cost of the life insurance you may wish to purchase.

The direct-response marketing system encourages you to calculate the amount of life insurance you need for family protection using the steps provided in Chapter Eight. Once the amount of life insurance is determined, you can refer to the schedules in Appendix E to compute the cost of no-commission term insurance and no-commission universal life insurance for your particular situation. Whether term or permanent insurance is most appropriate for your individual situation is discussed in Chapters Nine and Ten.

The advantages of buying no-commission term insurance is described in Chapter Six. The substantial economic advantages of buying no-commission universal life are demonstrated in Chapter Seven.

The other alternative to the commission-motivated system for selling life insurance is the fee-for-service delivery system. This system encourages life insurance consumers to contact a life insurance professional who is paid directly by the consumer rather than earning commissions paid by insurance companies for the sale of their policies.

The source of their compensation rewards fee-for-service life insurance advisers for providing objective information and advice that is focused on the client's best interests. For example, a fee-for-service life insurance adviser's recommendation to a wealthy client considering the purchase of life insurance to pay estate taxes may be to not buy life insurance at all, but to use other strategies - a recommendation a commission-motivated agent isn't likely to make. Commission-motivated agents are rewarded for selling life insurance policies, not for providing consumers with objective life insurance planning information.

Because fee-for-service life insurance advisers are independent with no financial interest in the client's purchase decisions, they offer consumers a significantly higher level of safety when recommending life insurance companies. Advisers don't work for any particular company, aren't influenced by the level of commissions a policy pays and are compensated for providing the client with cautious policy recommendations. Agents may ignore danger signals concerning a company's financial health if they are agents of the particular company, will receive a larger commission for selling one policy over another (one company that is in receivership paid local agents a first year commission of 80%) or are simply too busy soliciting to adequately research a recommended company's financial strength.

Also, fee-for-service advisers give their clients access to wholesale costs for their life insurance purchases by recommending low-load, no-commission policies whenever appropriate and possible. When a commission-paying policy is more appropriate, fee-for-service advisers help clients obtain better value for their money by restructuring the agent-sold policy to reduce commissions, when possible, and by recommending a full or significant commission rebate as allowed by law. This not only saves the client significant premium dollars, but guarantees that the fee-for-service life insurance adviser doesn't have a financial interest in any decision made by the client.

One of my pet peeves is reading or listening to arguments that merely state the obvious. However, at the risk of incurring your anger, I must state the obvious. Changing the source of the insurance adviser's compensation, from insurance companies' commissions to fees paid directly by the client, turns the client/insurance adviser relationship around 180 degrees. It is the only change in this relationship that can assure the client that he and the insurance adviser are on the same team working for the same goal - determining the most appropriate life insurance planning and purchases available to the client.

These two alternative systems for life insurance planning and purchasing policies at wholesale prices can handle any life insurance need that arises. For the vast majority of consumers, whose primary need for life insurance is to protect their families, the direct-response system is ideal. Fee-for- service life insurance advisers should be considered for two major purposes. First, they can assist you with the more complicated purchases of life insurance associated with estate planning and business planning. These issues are discussed in Chapters Twelve and Thirteen. And secondly, fee-for-service advisers are especially valuable in assisting you review the life insurance policies you already own. This issue is discussed in Chapter Fourteen.

If you would like to work with a fee-for-service life insurance adviser, you may contact the Life Insurance Advisers Association (LIAA) at their toll free number, 800-521-4578. The LIAA, of which I am a founding member, can put you in touch with a fee-for-service life insurance adviser on your request.

In later chapters I discuss the dramatic savings available when you purchase either no-commission term or no-commission universal life policies from either Ameritas or USAA. If only 10,000 astute life insurance consumers purchased their life insurance on a no-commission direct-response basis, rather than buying full-commission policies through life insurance agents, the combined savings this year alone would be roughly $20 million, and the savings would be $32.5 million over the first 10 years the policies were owned. And if each year, 10,000 consumers purchased no-commission term and universal life insurance, rather than commission paying policies, the cumulative savings after 10 years would be roughly $300 MILLION!!!

These figures are based on an average policy size of $600,000, and the average age of the insured at 38, with half buying no-commission term insurance and half buying no-commission universal life policies. These savings don't affect the insurance companies or the American economy. It is money consumers would save that could be spent or invested.

CHAPTER SIX

NO-COMMISSION TERM INSURANCE

This chapter describes the advantages of no-commission term insurance and Chapter Seven describes the advantages of no- commission universal life, both sold directly by Ameritas and USAA. First I will briefly describe the major reasons to purchase life insurance:

1. Family protection;
2. As an estate planning asset; and
3. To fund obligations associated with the transfer of a closely-held business.

Family protection refers to the purchase of life insurance to protect the family in the event of the death of the primary family income earners. This is discussed in Chapter Eight. Whether term or a permanent form of life insurance is most appropriate for family protection is described in Chapters Nine and Ten. For now, let me state that either term or permanent life insurance may be considered as an appropriate choice for family protection.

Life insurance used as an estate planning asset refers to buying life insurance to provide estate liquidity to pay estate taxes and other expenses or to equalize inheritances to heirs. Because the life insurance will be needed at death, permanent life insurance is the only appropriate choice. These issues are discussed in more detail in Chapter Twelve.

Life insurance used to fund obligations associated with the transfer of a closely-held business is used in conjunction with a buy-sell agreement between owners of a business. Either term or permanent life insurance would be considered appropriate for this purpose, depending on the circumstances, which are discussed in Chapter Thirteen.

While term insurance is a relatively simple concept to understand, the variety of term insurance policies sold can lead to considerable confusion. As described in Chapter One, term insurance is a pay-as-you-go life insurance policy that doesn't create a policy cash value. In theory, the insurance company charges a sufficient annual premium to cover anticipated death claims and to cover policy expenses. This obligation to pay a death claim and the cost of policy expenses is offset by the insurance company's earnings on the premiums collected and held until death claims are paid.

The marketing and selling of term insurance is competitive, as it should be. But, these competitive pressures encourage some insurance companies to design term insurance policies that contain certain hazards for the unsuspecting consumer. Essentially, there are two types of term insurance policy designs that can cause problems for consumers. One is a term policy having a very low rate the first year that rapidly increases in subsequent years. Many consumers pay much more attention to the premium rate they must pay now than to the premium rate two, three and more years away. This issue is explained in more detail in Appendix F.

The second term insurance policy design that can cause problems is a policy with very competitive rates for a specified period of time, after which the insured must be in the same health as when the policy was purchased or the rates will go up substantially. This type of policy is known as a re-entry policy. It is also discussed in more detail in Appendix F.

Neither Ameritas or USAA has designed their no-commission term policies with first-year low-ball rates followed by much higher rates or with a re-entry feature.

On a level playing field term life insurance policies ought to be priced based on:

1. Adequate and conservative medical evaluation of each potential insured;

2. Cost of insurance rates based on actual industry mortality experience;

3. Prudent expectations of investment returns, which are based on a prudent investment portfolio; and

4. Full recognition and recovery of policy expenses.

Many life insurance companies, including Ameritas and USAA, offering term insurance have used similar pricing parameters, therefore the outstanding pricing difference between other companies and Ameritas and USAA is in the area of policy expenses.

Both the no-commission term insurance policies sold on a direct basis by Ameritas and USAA have considerably lower policy sales charges than their full-commission term insurance counterparts, which translates into lower policy pricing. The largest policy expenses associated with the sale of full-commission term insurance policies are the commissions paid to the selling agent and his general agent, which combined will generally be in the range of 70% to 90% of the first-year premium. Combined renewal commissions are between 5% to 15% of subsequent premiums for four to nine years, depending on the particular policy sold. Ameritas has built into their no-commission term policy an expense of 32% of the first-year premium and 2% thereafter. USAA has not disclosed to me the expenses associated with the sale of their no-commission term insurance policy, but they have indicated they are similar to those of the Ameritas term policy.

However, the pricing advantage for low-load term insurance policies assumes a level playing field, which isn't always the case. As described earlier, creative term insurance policy designs can make the playing field uneven.

Therefore, listing the lowest-priced term insurance rates available isn't appropriate for this book because there are frequently hazards that consumers may have difficulty detecting. Also, term insurance rates change so frequently any listing would be quickly outdated.

Another reason to buy the term insurance you may require on a no-commission direct-response basis from Ameritas or USAA is because I believe it is to your advantage to eliminate the need to deal with commission-motivated life insurance agents. Each agent has his own agenda and strongly held ideas about the kind of life insurance their customers should purchase (see Appendix C). You simply can't be assured that the life insurance agent's agenda will serve what is in your best interests. The only way you can be assured your best interests are being represented is to take control of your own life insurance agenda and buy your life insurance directly, or retain the services of a fee-for-service life insurance adviser who will help you purchase a no-commission life insurance policy.

I don't, however, claim that there aren't lower priced full-commission term policies than the no-commission term policies offered directly by Ameritas and USAA. Some insurance companies offer term policies that are very low priced as a loss leader. Generally, companies offer these very low-priced term policies in anticipation that enough of these policies will be converted to their permanent policies, which are very profitable. If you are determined to find the lowest-priced term insurance policy possible, you are advised to contact as many insurance agents as it takes for you to be satisfied.

The Ameritas no-commission term policy is a five-year level policy. That is, the quoted premium remains level for five years, and increases in five-year increments. The premium rate is guaranteed for the first three years. After three years the premium rate could go up or down. Any such increases or decreases would occur at the beginning of a new policy year and would apply to all policies in that particular class of policies.

The Ameritas no-commission five-year level term policy may be renewed every five years until age 80 without new evidence of insurability. This policy doesn't require re-entry. It may be exchanged for an Ameritas no-commission universal life policy without proof of insurability during the first five years.

After five years, a medical exam would be necessary to exchange the no-commission five-year level term policy for a no- commission universal life policy.

The Ameritas no-commission five-year level term policy has three basic premium rate classifications. For non-smokers, there are preferred and standard classifications. For smokers, there is only a standard rate classification. Besides the standard classifications, there are special rates for individuals who have one or more health problems that would prevent them from being classified as standard. The amount of the sub-standard rate will be indicated by Ameritas when a policy is issued.

The Ameritas no-commission five-year level term premium rate schedule, found on pages 145-47, lists the requirements to qualify for a preferred non-smoker classification. If you meet all of the requirements listed, you should use the preferred rate. If you don't meet all the requirements, you should use their standard rate. But keep in mind that the actual premium rate you will be charged won't be known until the policy is issued by Ameritas because your rate will depend on your overall health status, which will be reviewed by them.

The term policy offered by USAA is an annual renewal term policy. This means that the term premium will go up each year. The USAA term premium is guaranteed for one year and could be increased or decreased thereafter. Any increase or decrease would occur at the beginning of a new policy year and would apply to all policies in that particular class of policies. USAA has sold this no-commission term policy for seven years and has experienced two rate reductions. The USAA no- commission annual renewal term rates are found on pages 148-49.

The USAA no-commission annual renewal term policy may be renewed to age 70. New evidence of insurability is not required to continue the policy. You may exchange a USAA no-commission annual renewal term policy for their no-commission universal life policy without proof of insurability any time to age 70.

USAA's no-commission annual renewal term policy has two basic rate classifications: standard non-smoker and standard smoker. As is the case with Ameritas, there are special rates for individuals with one or more health problems. These higher sub-standard premium rates are declared by USAA when the policy is issued.

In summary, my recommendation that you purchase the term insurance you may require from Ameritas and USAA on a direct, no-commission basis is because both companies have the highest A.M. Best rating, they have made realistic cost of insurance assumptions and have prudent investment portfolios. The outstanding difference in their favor is the significantly lower policy acquisition expenses that are possible because the policies can be purchased on a direct basis, sans life insurance agent.

CHAPTER SEVEN

No-Commission Universal Life

Universal life insurance is one of the various types of permanent insurance. Permanent forms of life insurance generate a policy surplus, or cash value, in addition to a death benefit. The primary reason for purchasing a permanent insurance policy is to avoid the very high annual term insurance premiums as the insured approaches life expectancy. As described in Chapter One, the permanent insurance annual premium is set up to remain level throughout the insured's life. This level premium in the early years is in excess of the actual cost of insurance and policy expenses. This higher premium creates the policy cash value, which reduces the risk portion (total death benefit less the policy's cash value) of the policy subject to the higher cost of insurance rates as the insured gets older. That is, if the permanent policy's death benefit is $500,000 with a $100,000 cash value, the actual risk portion is $400,000 ($500,000 - $100,000).

Unlike some other forms of permanent insurance, universal life policies are very flexible and don't require a specified annual premium based on the amount of death benefit, or the insured's age and health status. Rather, universal life policies are similar to buying term insurance with a separate cash value account. The annual premium in excess of the cost of insurance and policy expenses is credited to the cash value account and earns interest at the rate declared by the insurance company.

I recommend purchasing a universal life policy based on a concept known as "endowment at age 95." Endowment at age 95 means that the cash value and death benefit are approximately equal at age 95. This is the true definition of a permanent life insurance policy. The practical application of buying a universal life policy that endows at age 95 is described later in this chapter.

Expenses are a major pricing component associated with a permanent life insurance policy. By far the largest expense is the commissions that are paid to the selling agent and his general agent. These combined commissions are generally in the range of 90% to 110% of the first-year premium. Also, the insurance company accrues a percentage of the premiums they receive for marketing purposes, generally referred to as a marketing allowance. The combined first-year distribution costs, therefore, are usually 110% to 125% of the first-year premium for agent-sold, full-commission permanent insurance policies. In addition, there are renewal commissions paid to the agent and his general agent, which are 5% to 20% of subsequent premiums for a period of four to nine years, depending on the particular policy sold. After renewal commissions are no longer paid the agent and general agent typically receive a combined 4% of all subsequent premiums.

While no-commission universal life policies have no agent commission expenses, there are acquisition costs. Ameritas has acquisition costs built into its no-commission universal life policies of 16% of the target premium. Renewal expenses are 2% of subsequent premiums. USAA hasn't disclosed their universal life acquisition costs, but indicated they are very similar to those of Ameritas.

The drastic difference in policy acquisition costs between full-commission and no-commission universal life policies produces a significant premium savings when a policy is purchased from either Ameritas or USAA.

Equally important as the premium savings possible with a no-commission universal life policy is the immediate cash value it generates because of the dramatically lower first-year acquisition costs. The importance of this immediate cash value is highlighted by the alarming number of permanent life insurance policies that are canceled. You will recall from the Introduction the 1990

LIMRA study which found that nearly half of permanent policies purchased will be canceled within the first seven years. Cancellation of full-commission permanent policies in such a short period of time has extremely negative economic consequences for consumers because it takes full-commission permanent policies at least 10 years to fully amortize the very high first-year acquisition costs. This amortization of sales charges has a direct effect on the policy cash value.

Several examples will demonstrate the advantages of a lower premium and immediate cash value available with no-commission universal life policies compared to full-commission permanent life insurance policies. The next chapter describes a relatively simple method for calculating the amount of family protection life insurance you may require. In the narrative explaining this method, I have taken a theoretical family through the process of determining the amount of family protection life insurance they may need. This theoretical family determines, based on the calculations in Chapter Eight, that the primary income earner requires additional life insurance on his life of $600,000. He is a 38-year-old, non- smoker in good health.

Exhibit 7-1, on page 56, represents a $600,000 Ameritas no-commission universal life policy illustration for our theoretical primary family income earner. The annual target premium of $2,623 is based on generating a cash value of $600,000 at age 95, assuming current cost of insurance and an interest credited rate of 8.5%. Note the cash value at the end of the first year and thereafter.

Exhibit 7-2, on page 56, is a full-commission universal life policy illustration for a 38-year-old male, non-smoker in good health with a $600,000 death benefit. The annual premium of $5,920 the first year and $3,150 thereafter is based on generating an identical cash value ($71,934) in 20 years as is generated for the no-commission universal life policy illustration in Exhibit 7-1. The full-commission universal life proposal illustration also has an interest credited rate of 8.5%. Note the absence of any cash

EXHIBIT 7-1

AMERITAS NO-COMMISSION UNIVERSAL LIFE

Death Benefit: $600,000   Age: 38 Male Non-Smoker

Interest Credited Asumption: 8.5%

Age	Annual Premium	Cumulative Premiums Paid	Cash Value	Death Benefit
38	$2,623	$2,623	$2,280	$600,000
39	"	5,246	4,383	"
40	"	7,869	6,421	"
41	"	10,492	8,420	"
42	"	13,115	10,343	"
47	"	26,230	23,455	"
52	"	39,345	44,470	"
57	"	52,460	71,934	"
95	"	149,511	600,000	606,000

EXHIBIT 7-2

FULL-COMMISSION UNIVERSAL LIFE

Death Benefit: $600,000   Age: 38 Male Non-Smoker

Interest Credited Asumption: 8.5%

Age	Annual Premium	Cumulative Premiums Paid	Cash Value	Death Benefit
38	$5,920	$5,920	0	$600,000
39	3,150	9,070	0	"
40	"	12,226	4,958	"
41	"	15,325	7,570	"
42	"	18,475	10,335	"
47	"	34,270	26,519	"
52	"	50,020	46,836	"
57	"	65,770	71,934	"

value in the first two years.

The distribution expenses for the Ameritas policy in Exhibit 7-1 are: $420 the first year; $420 the second year; $383 the third year; and $52 each year thereafter. This is in contrast to the first-year acquisition costs for the agent-sold, full-commission universal life policy illustration in Exhibit 7-2 of nearly $7,400, with subsequent expenses of $315 annually for nine years, followed by $125 annually thereafter.

An agent selling the full-commission universal life policy in exhibit 7-2 would earn a commission in the first year of approximately $3,250, and his general agent would earn approximately the same amount. It is common for the general agent to pay the agent a bonus commission from his commissions if the agent has reached established production targets. This bonus commission is generally 15% of the first-year premium. Therefore, an agent might except to earn total commissions for the sale of the policy illustrated in Exhibit 7-2 of approximately $4,100.

Exhibit 7-3 combines the information from Exhibits 7-1 and 7-2 to more readily demonstrate the significant economic advantages of no-commission universal life.

EXHIBIT 7-3

| Death Benefit: $600,000 | | | Age: 38 Male Non-Smoker | |
| Full-Commission Policy | | | No-Commission Policy | |
Age	Cumulative Premiums	Cash Value	Cumulative Premiums	Cash Value
38	$5,920	0	$2,623	$2,280
39	9,070	0	5,246	4,383
40	12,226	4,958	7,869	6,421
41	15,325	7,570	10,429	8,420
42	18,475	10,335	13,118	10,343
47	34,279	26,519	26,230	23,455
52	50,020	46,836	39,345	44,470
57	65,770	71,934	52,460	71,934

The no-commission universal life policy (Exhibit 7-1) is projected to require cumulative premiums of $52,460 over 20 years to generate a cash value of $71,934. In contrast, the full-commission policy (Exhibit 7-2) is projected to require cumulative premiums of $65,770 over 20 years to arrive at an identical cash value of $71,934. This is a cumulative premium difference of $13,310, which is the projected net savings after 20 years for astute consumers buying no-commission UL. If these net savings were invested at 8% after-tax, the invested value of the annual premium differences between the no-commission and full-commission after 20 years is nearly $39,000.

The no-commission universal life policies sold directly by Ameritas and USAA have a significant advantage in drastically reducing the policy distribution expenses. This provides the policyholder with an immediate policy cash value and the potential that the policy's cash value, when the premiums are the same, will be superior to full-commission alternatives over an extended period of time. Glenn S. Daily, in his book The *Individual Investor's Guide To Low-Load Insurance Products*, calculates that in order for a full-load permanent policy to overcome a low-load policy's expense advantages, it would need to credit 1.4% to 1.5% greater interest per year than a low-load policy. This is very unlikely because most life insurance companies invest the majority of the premiums they collect in intermediate-term high-grade corporate and government securities. To invest otherwise exposes their investment portfolio to considerably more risk. Insurance companies that have invested in more risky investments, such as junk bonds and real estate, are paying a heavy price in consumer confidence.

Regarding the purchase of no-commission universal life, when you call Ameritas, USAA, or both, ask for a proposal illustration in which the annual target premium is determined based on the policy endowing at age 95. The proposal illustration will calculate the target premium assuming the current cost of insurance and interest credited rates. The annual target premium will be based on creating a sufficient surplus to produce the endowment at age 95.

The proposal illustration will not be guaranteed since it is based on current cost of insurance and interest credited assumptions. This is why it is called a "target" premium: It is the estimated annual premium necessary to accomplish the goal of endowment at age 95 based on current assumptions for cost of insurance and interest credited rates.

If you purchase a no-commission universal life policy, compare the annual statements you will receive at each policy anniversary with the original proposal illustration. As interest credited rates fluctuate - and they will - you will notice a difference between the actual cash value and the projected cash value from the original proposal illustration. The actual cash value may be larger or smaller than the original proposal illustration. Every two or three years, ask the insurance company to send you a new proposal illustration based on your actual cash value. This new illustration will compute a new annual target premium needed to endow the policy at age 95 based on the actual cash value, current cost of insurance and interest credited rates. This is what I do for my clients.

Tracking the actual cost of insurance rates with the projected cost of insurance rates will be very difficult and is not necessary if you request a new proposal illustration every two or three years. The new proposal illustrations will take into consideration any changes in current and projected cost of insurance rates. Neither Ameritas nor USAA has ever raised their projected cost of insurance rates for their no-commission universal life policies.

As stated earlier, no-commission universal life policies are very flexible. You can adjust the amount of annual premium you wish to pay, reduce or increase (with proof of good health) the death benefit, and withdraw cash value. For example, if you purchase a no-commission universal life policy and have a job in which your compensation fluctuates, you could pay additional premiums in the good years and pay a lower or no premium in down years. With some other forms of permanent insurance, if an annual premium isn't made it must be covered from the policy cash value. This creates a loan in which annual interest would be due. Missing a premium with a universal life policy doesn't create a loan.

Keep in mind, however, that this flexibility is a two-edged sword. You can lose track of how your policy is performing relative to your original goal. This is why it is so important to obtain a new proposal illustration every two or three years.

The monitoring of a no-commission universal life policy may leave you confused. A fee-for-service life insurance adviser can assist you in this monitoring, if you choose to retain one.

The next three chapters will help you understand the role no-commission term and universal life policies, offered on a direct basis by Ameritas and USAA, can play in your personal need for life insurance, and help you decide whether no-commission term or no-commission universal life is best for you.

CHAPTER EIGHT

FAMILY PROTECTION LIFE INSURANCE

In Chapter Two I made the claim that one of the problems with the commission-motivated system for selling life insurance is that many consumers don't intend to buy it. Life insurance is sold, not bought. Most families don't decide to prospectively analyze their needs for life insurance. Rather, they are solicited by an insurance agent.

All too often life insurance is purchased for its presumed investment potential, or simply because it is marketed as a good buy. What is missing frequently is a rational basis for the purchase of life insurance.

Astute consumers of life insurance should begin by recognizing that there are only three basic needs for life insurance:

1. Family protection;
2. As an estate planning asset; and
3. To fund obligations associated with the transfer of a closely-held business.

These basic needs for life insurance are better understood if you realize that what we are really talking about is 'death' insurance. Life insurance isn't an investment - it is primarily a risk management asset.

For most consumers the major reason to purchase life insurance is to provide family protection in the event the primary family income earner has the bad judgment to die. This chapter describes a fairly simple method for determining how much family protection life insurance is appropriate. Life insurance used as an estate planning asset is described in Chapter Twelve. Chapter Thirteen discusses life insurance used to fund obligations associated with the transfer of a closely-held business.

There are many different methods for determining the amount of family protection life insurance needed. Some of them are rather complicated and require a computer program or at least complex formulas. The one I will share with you is very simple.

After all, complicated spreadsheet formats that take into account every conceivable variable will produce an insurance amount no more accurate than the most arbitrary variable. Let's not kid ourselves, the amount of life insurance purchased for family protection is at best a good guess. This is not like trying to get a rocket to the moon.

This system for determining the amount of life insurance necessary is based on the theory that you need a principal amount that can be invested to produce annual income sufficient to provide financial security for your family. That is, if your family protection income goal is $50,000 annually, and you believe that an 8% investment return is achievable, there must be a sum of $625,000 available to be invested in the event of your death. This is determined by dividing the annual income you want available for your family, in this case $50,000, by the assumed investment return rate of 8%. $50,000 divided by 0.08 = $625,000.

I will go through the process of determining the amount of life insurance needed for family protection in a narrative form. I will ask questions and answer them as you might answer them. The figures used are merely examples to better explain the process. At the end of this chapter is a worksheet completed as the theoretical couple in the narrative would have completed it. In the back of this book is a worksheet you may use for determining your own family protection life insurance needs. Don't be intimidated by the length of the worksheet. Its format is intended to simplify the process by providing instructions for each component.

The first question to answer is: How much income does your

family need on a monthly basis in the event of your demise? Start with a monthly amount that allows you to think in terms of your everyday financial obligations. Let's say you determine that your family needs $5,000 per month on a pretax basis.

The next step is to list monthly income sources available, even if you are deceased, that may be used to offset this goal of $5,000 per month.

For example, your spouse may earn $1,000 per month at a part- time job. Whether or not this amount should be used to offset the $5,000 goal depends on if you want the flexibility for your spouse to be able to stay home because of the added responsibility of being a widowed parent. You decide you don't want to offset this $1,000 against your $5,000 monthly survivor's income goal.

Next, if you have children under 18, do you want to use Social Security payments, which may amount to $700 per month per child under 18 (up to a maximum of two children), as an offset? Again the important issue is flexibility. You decide you will disregard Social Security payments as an offset to your $5,000 monthly survivor's goal.

Five thousand dollars per month on an annualized basis is $60,000. The next question to answer is: What investment rate of return do you want to assume for a principal amount invested to produce $60,000 annually?

Remember that the $5,000 per month was on a pretax basis, so the assumed investment rate is based on a pretax basis as well. You determine that 8.0% is a reasonable investment rate assumption. Therefore, you need a fund of $750,000 ($60,000 divided by 0.08) that invested at 8%, will yield an annual return of $60,000. This $750,000 is called the survivor's principal goal.

To demonstrate how the decisions and the assumed investment rate will affect our survivor's principal goal, let's change them.

If our decision had been to offset the spouse's income of $1,000 and Social Security of approximately $700 per child (assuming two children under 18, 2 x $700, or $1,400), our survivor's monthly income goal would have been $2,600 ($5,000 - $2,400), or $31,200 annually ($2,600 x 12). With an 8% investment return assumption the principal goal would change to $390,000 ($31,200 divided by 0.08). And if the investment return assumption were 10% rather than 8%, the principal amount would be $312,000 ($31,200 divided by 0.10).

Does the $5,000 per month goal take into consideration funding such goals as education for the children and other financial goals you wish your family to continue striving for? For example, you may wish to provide additional funding for college education by making an assumption about its future cost. If you have determined that based on today's cost it will take $16,000 for four years of college for each of your two children, with the first starting in five years and the other in seven years, then you can compute the future value needed based on your estimation of educational cost inflation. For example, the future value of $16,000, assuming a 5% inflation rate, in five years is approximately $20,000, and $23,000 in seven years. Therefore, you should consider increasing the principal amount needed by $43,000, which increases the survivor's principal goal to $793,000, ($750,000 + $43,000).

What other factors should you consider? Perhaps the mortgage balance on your residence or on a vacation home should be considered for additional funding. If the monthly mortgage payments could be managed with the $5,000 per month survivor's income goal, then additional principal may not be needed. For our example you decide to disregard these mortgage needs.

Based on our scenario to this point, you have determined that you require a survivor's fund of $793,000. The next step is to determine whether you wish to factor into this process future inflation. Considering that the survivor's income goal is being funded with a principal amount intended to produce that income, most clients choose to ignore future inflation because the principal can provide additional support if it is needed. However, if inflation is important for you, you can increase the survivor's principal goal by an amount you feel will provide an inflation cushion. For example, you may wish to increase the survivor's principal goal by 20% to $900,000, ($750,000 x 1.2, not $793,000 x 1.2, since the educational fund of $43,000 has already been adjusted for assumed inflation).

For this example, let's assume that you decline considering future inflation. Therefore, your survivor's principal goal is still $793,000. The next step is to subtract from this amount assets presently available to meet this goal. You have $100,000 of participating group life insurance from your employer, a vested pension fund of $43,000 and invested assets of $50,000 for a total of $193,000. Therefore, your life insurance deficit is $600,000 ($793,000 - $193,000).

However we're not finished yet. What about the untimely demise of your spouse, who earns $1,000 per month and provides the majority of care for your two children? How would her demise affect the family financial condition? You decide that not only do you wish to provide for her lost income but also the additional cost for a housekeeper at a cost of $1,000 per month. Therefore, you require principal funding for $2,000 per month, or $24,000 annually. Again, assuming an 8.0% investment return, the principal amount needed is $300,000 ($24,000 divided by 0.08). The final step, as before, is to subtract from this $300,000 goal assets presently available. You have invested assets of $50,000 and a whole life policy insuring your wife for $10,000, for a total of $60,000. This leaves an unfunded balance of $240,000 ($300,000 - $60,000), which is the amount of life insurance required for your spouse.

Summary of Steps for Determining Family Protection Life Insurance

1. Decide the amount of monthly family income required in the event of the demise of either spouse. This is the survivor's monthly income goal.
2. Subtract from this survivor's monthly income goal the amount of income that would be available.
3. Select a return on investment assumption.
4. Annualize the monthly survivor's income goal and divide by the return on investment assumption. This is the survivor's principal goal.
5. Add to this survivor's principal goal other financial goals you wish to fund (e.g., college education) on a future value basis.
6. Although most clients ignore future inflation in this system for determining family protection life insurance needs, if it is important to you, increase the survivor's principal goal as a cushion against inflation.
7. Subtract from the survivor's principal goal assets which are presently available (e.g., life insurance, pension funds, investments, etc.). The result is the amount of life insurance needed.

Our theoretical couple's worksheet is shown on the following pages.

FAMILY PROTECTION LIFE INSURANCE CALCULATION WORKSHEET
FOR THE PRIMARY INCOME EARNER

STEP 1:

Decide the amount of monthly income, on a pretax basis, your family will need if you are deceased <u>5,000</u> (line 1). This is the survivor's monthly income goal.

STEP 2:

Subtract from the amount in line 1 income, on a monthly basis, available to meet this survivor's monthly income goal.

Surviving spouse's monthly income	_____
Social Security (dependent children or other categories)	_____
Pension benefits payable	_____
Other	_____
	_____
	_____
	_____
	_____
Total (line 2)	_____

(Note: You may wish to ignore any or all of these income sources to provide your survivors with more income and therefore, more flexibility. Cross out sources of monthly income you don't wish to consider.)

Subtract from line 1	<u>5,000</u>
Amount on line 2	_____
Survivor's Monthly Income Goal (line 3)	<u>5,000</u>

STEP 3:

To express the survivor's monthly income goal on an annual basis, multiply line 3 by 12.

(line 3)	<u>5,000</u>
	x 12
Survivor's Annual Income Goal (line 4)	<u>60,000</u>

STEP 4:

Select an assumed investment rate of return on a pretax basis.

(line 5) <u>8.0 %</u>

Move the decimal point for the assumed investment rate in line 5 two places to the left. (line 6) <u>.08</u>

Divide line 4 by line 6.

    60,000 divided by ·08   = (line 7) 750,000
The result in line 7 is the Survivor's Principal Goal.

STEP 5:

If you wish to provide additional funding for future inflation you may
increase the survivor's principal goal from line 9 by some percentage -
10%, 20%, 30% etc. This may not be necessary because principal could be
used for additional support if needed. Also if you review your family
protection needs every two years this will tend to offset the need to estimate future inflation.

          Survivor's Principal Goal   (line 7) 750,000
          Inflation factor   x 1.0
          (For example, 20% would be 1.20)
          Survivor's Principal Goal   (line 8) 750,000

STEP 6:

List financial obligations you would like to fund. (Note: Obligations such
as mortgages, which are being paid off with monthly payments, may not
need additional funding if your survivor's monthly income goal will cover
these monthly payments. Obligations such as college education for children may be expressed either in present value dollars or at their estimated
future value.)

          College education fund   43,000
          Other

                                             _____
                                             _____
                                             _____
                                             _____

          Total   (line 9) 43,000

          Add line 9 and   43,000
          line 8   750,000

          Survivor's Principal Goal   (line 10) 793,000
STEP 7:

Reduce the survivor's principal goal by assets presently available to fund
this goal.

Life insurance	100,000
Vested pension funds	43,000
Personal investments	50,000
Other	

Total	(line 11)	193,000
Subtract from line 10		793,000
amount on line 11		193,000

Survivor's Principal Goal Deficit   600,000

This is a 'rough estimate' of the amount of life insurance that should be purchased for the primary income earner. To further simplify this process, skip steps 2, 5 and 6.

FAMILY PROTECTION LIFE INSURANCE CALCULATION WORKSHEET FOR PRIMARY INCOME EARNER'S SPOUSE

STEP 1:

Decide the amount of monthly income, on a pretax basis, that would be lost if the primary income earner's spouse were deceased.

(line 1) 1,000

Determine the additional monthly expenses that would be incurred if the primary income earner's spouse were deceased.

(line 2) 1,000

Add lines 1 and 2.

Survivor's Monthly Income Goal   (line 3) 2,000

STEP 2:

To express the survivor's monthly income goal on an annual basis, multiply line 3 by 12.

(line 3) 2,000
x12

Survivor's Annual Income Goal   (line 4) 24,000

STEP 3:

Select an assumed investment rate of return, on a pretax basis.

(line 5) __8.0 %__

Move the decimal point for the assumed investment rate in line 5 two places to the left.   (line 6) __.08__

Divide line 4 by line 6.

__24,000__ divided by __.08__ = (line 7) 300,000

The result on line 7 is the survivor's principal goal.

STEP 4:

Reduce the survivor's principal goal by assets presently available to fund this goal.

Life insurance	10,000
Pension funds	
Personal investments	50,000
Other	
Total	(line 8) 60,000
Subtract from line 7	300,000
amount on line 8	60,000
Survivor's Principal Goal Deficit	240,000

This is a 'rough estimate' of life insurance that should be purchased for the primary income earner's spouse.

A blank worksheet is included in the back of the book for your family protection life insurance calculations.

CHAPTER NINE

TERM OR PERMANENT INSURANCE I

If family protection is your primary need for life insurance and you have determined the amount for yourself, and perhaps for your spouse, by using the Family Protection Life Insurance Calculation Worksheet, your next step is to determine the cost of no-commission term insurance and compare it with the cost of no-commission universal life. This comparison is initially done with the information provided in this chapter and Appendix E. The only purpose for this initial comparison is to determine whether your budget can afford the higher universal life premium. Regardless of whether your choice is no- commission term or universal life, you should contact Ameritas, USAA, or both for proposal illustrations for the policy (or policies) you wish to purchase.

To pick up from our example in Chapter Eight, our primary family income earner, whom we will now call John, has determined that he needs to purchase a life insurance policy for $600,000 and one for his spouse for $240,000. John is a 38-year-old non-smoker who meets the requirements established by Ameritas to qualify for a preferred non-smoker rate. His wife is a 35-year-old non-smoker who also qualifies for a preferred rate. John can compute the projected five-year level term premiums for his wife and himself by using the premium rate schedule for the Ameritas no-commission five-year level term shown in Appendix E.

I have used the Ameritas no-commission five-year level term policy for my comparisons in this chapter and in Chapter Ten because the premium increases in five-year increments rather than every year, and therefore it is easier to compute the relative economic differences between buying no-commission term insurance and buying a no-commission universal life policy. I have no preference between the Ameritas no-commission five-year level term and USAA's no-commission annual renewal term policy. Whether Ameritas or USAA has the lower rate for your personal situation will depend on your age and if you qualify for the preferred non-smoker rating with Ameritas.

I urge you to take the time to calculate premium rates for both the Ameritas five-year level term and USAA's annual renewal term for your individual situation. This term insurance premium comparison can only be done for a five-year period because the Ameritas rate schedule in Appendix E can only be used for the first five years. To determine the rate for subsequent five- year periods you must contact Ameritas and have them send you a proposal illustration for their five-year level term policy.

John calculates the projected five-year level term rate from Ameritas for his $600,000 policy to be $702. This is done by multiplying the per $1,000 rate of $1.17 on page 147 by the number of $1,000 units John is purchasing, which is 600. He calculates the projected five-year level term rate from Ameritas for his wife to be $233 for her $240,000 term policy. This was calculated by multiplying the per $1,000 rate of $0.97 found on page 147 by 240, the number of $1,000 units being purchased.

Once you have determined the lowest term premium rate available to you, you should compare it with the premium rate for a no- commission universal life policy also found in Appendix E at pages 152-53. Ameritas has provided me with the projected rate for their no-commission universal life policy based on an interest credited rate of 8.0% and their current cost of insurance rate for a policy that will endow at age 95. You recall from Chapter Seven that endowing at 95 means that the cash value and death benefit are approximately equal at age 95. This premium rate is expressed as a cost per $1,000.

John's projected annual premium for an Ameritas $600,000 no-commission universal life policy, based on the specifications mentioned in the previous paragraph, is a rate per $1,000 of $4.78, or a projected annual premium of approximately $2,868 ($4.78 x 600). The projected cost for his wife is a rate per $1,000 of $3.08, or a projected annual premium of $739 (3.08 x 240) for a no-commission universal life policy for $240,000.

The only reason these Ameritas no-commission universal life rates are provided and this comparison made is to determine whether this family's budget can afford the higher annual premiums for the no-commission universal life policies. They can now decide whether the five-year level term premium of $702 or the universal life premium of $2,868 for his policy and the five-year level term premium of $233 or the universal life premium of $739 for her policy are more compatible with their budget.

If a no-commission universal life policy from either Ameritas or USAA is even being considered, you must call them and order a proposal illustration using my suggestions in Chapter Seven.

If our theoretical couple decided that their budget just simply couldn't handle the higher no-commission universal life insurance premiums, their life insurance planning would be nearly completed.

The important point is that John and his wife purchase the amount of family protection life insurance calculated in Chapter Eight. Even if John believed that no-commission universal life is a better value (discussed in Chapter Ten), he should not reduce the amount of life insurance protection to correspond with what his budget can afford in order to purchase no-commission universal life.

If you have decided, based solely on cost, that no-commission term insurance is the life insurance you will buy, you should call Ameritas and USAA and request that they send you term insurance proposal illustrations. Based on these proposal illustrations, you can determine which policy has the best projected pricing. Perhaps the easiest way to make this determination is to simply add up the projected premiums for a 10-year period of time. Or, if you are able to do present value calculations, you may wish to compare the present value of these premiums for 10 years.

Once you have decided whether you wish to buy the Ameritas five-year level term or the USAA annual renewal term policy, you should determine whether you are entitled to purchase group life insurance from an association you or your spouse may belong to. For example, if either of you is an attorney, accountant, dentist, physician, engineer, etc., there is generally group life insurance available through associations of these professional groups. If an association group life insurance plan is available to you, you should compare the unit cost of the group plan with the unit cost for the no-commission term insurance premium of the policy you have selected.

One caution about association group life insurance: If you leave the association, your group term insurance will be terminated. However, most association group plans will allow you to convert to a permanent policy. If you are in an association in which you might possibly terminate your membership, don't buy life insurance from their group plan.

Most likely the association group insurance and the no-commission term will be for a dissimilar amount of death benefit. To convert an association group insurance plan and no-commission term quote to a unit cost for a direct comparison, you need to:

1. Divide the amount of life insurance quoted by 1,000. This will give you the amount of $1,000 units being compared. $600,000 divided by $1,000 = 600 $1,000 units;

2. Divide the annual premium by the number of $1,000 units you are purchasing. $702 divided by 600 = $1.17 per $1,000.

These steps will give you the unit (per thousand) cost which makes a direct unit cost comparison of dissimilar amounts of life insurance possible. Exhibit 9-1 is an example of this method.

Two variables must be kept in mind. First, you must convert the quote to an annual premium. That is, if the premium is quoted as a semiannual premium, you must multiply it by two. Secondly, you must take into consideration the period of time the premium rate is for. For example, it may be for one year, five years or for a specified age period of say, 36 to 40 years of age.

Exhibit 9-1

XYZ Group Association
Maximum Group Term Insurance Amount Available - $250,000
Semiannual premium rate for male non-smokers ages 36 to 40
$200.00 for $250,000
Semiannual premium rate for male non-smokers ages 41 to 45
$300.00 for $250,000

Step 1   Multiply $200.00 by 2 = $400.00, to establish annual premium amount to age 40. Multiply $300.00 by 2 = $600.00, to establish annual premium amount from ages 41 to 45.

Step 2   Divide $250,000 by $1,000 = 250, to determine the number of $1,000 units.

Step 3   Divide the annual premium of $400.00 by the number of $1,000 units, $400 divided by 250 = $1.60, which is the projected unit cost per $1,000 of the XYZ group association life insurance for ages 36 to 40. Divide the annual premium of $600.00 by the number of $1,000 units, $600 divided by 250 = $2.40, which is the projected unit cost per $1,000 for ages 41 to 45.

Ameritas offers a $600,000 no-commission five-year level term insurance policy for John, who is 38 and a non-smoker in good health, for a projected five-year level annual premium of $702 for the first five years and $965 for a second five-year period.*

Step 1   (Premium is already expressed as an annual premium)

Step 2   Divide $600,000 by $1,000 = 600, to determine the number of $1,000 units.

Step 3   Divide the annual premium of $702 by the number of
          $1,000 units, $702 divided by 600 = $1.17, which is the projected unit
          cost of life insurance for the first five years. Divide the annual
          premium for the second five-year period of $965.00 by 600 = $1.61,
          which is the projected unit cost of life insurance for a second five
          years.

* The projected premium for a second five year period is obtained from a
proposal illustration sent out by Ameritas. This information isn't available in
the rate charts in Appendix E.

Obviously, the Ameritas no-commission five-year level term
policy has the lower unit cost.

If the association group insurance had a lower unit cost for
a similar period of time, John would purchase the group association insurance if he were reasonably certain he would remain in
the association. If, as in our example, the maximum amount of
group insurance available were $250,000 and the need is for
$600,000, then John would purchase $250,000 of group association term insurance and the difference, $350,000, from Ameritas.

At this point John has determined:

1. Based on the calculation in Chapter Eight, that he has a
   life insurance deficit of $600,000;
2. The best no-commission term insurance premium is a
   five-year level term policy;
3. Based on the relationship of the no-commission five-
   year level term insurance premium to the no-commission universal life premium, the family budget can't
   afford the higher universal life premiums; and
4. The XYZ association group term insurance plan premium is higher on a unit cost basis than the no-commission five-year level term unit cost.

John now has complete control of his life insurance planning.

For the most part, the steps presented in Chapter Eight and
in this chapter will allow you to have access to the direct-
response life insurance system. By using these steps, you will be

able to avoid the negative aspects of the commission-driven life insurance delivery system.

Two important items that you must consider when completing the no-commission term life insurance application (or any application for that matter) for Ameritas or USAA are who will own the policy and who will be designated as the policy beneficiary.

There are some creative planning opportunities available to you if you wish to retain an attorney to draft certain trust agreements to provide for management of the insurance proceeds in the event of your death. Such advice and drafting would cost you approximately $500 to $800 in legal fees. You should carefully read the first part of Chapter Twelve before deciding who will be beneficiary of your policy. If after reading Chapter Twelve you are unconvinced that executing a revocable trust is in your best interest, in most cases each spouse should own the policy insuring his or her own life and the beneficiary should be the other spouse, with the contingent beneficiaries being your "children equally, per stirpes." "Per stirpes" is a designation providing that if a child beneficiary has predeceased the insured, their share of the proceeds will go to any children they may have. If you don't have children other family members should be the contingent beneficiaries.

For consumers who have adequate cash flow to consider purchasing a no-commission universal life policy, the next chapter discusses a method of comparing the relative value of no-commission term insurance with that of no-commission universal life.

CHAPTER TEN

TERM OR PERMANENT INSURANCE II

This chapter compares the relative economic value of no-commission term insurance with that of no-commission universal life. Essentially, a comparison of the economic value of either purchase decision must focus on the difference in their annual premiums. For an extended period, the no-commission term insurance annual premium will be substantially less than the annual premium for a no-commission universal life policy for an equivalent amount of death benefit. But, the no-commission universal life policy generates a cash value, which the no-commission term policy doesn't. Therefore, a comparison can be made by subtracting the term insurance premium from the universal life premium and investing this difference in a theoretical investment fund, earning a specified rate of return. The value of this theoretical investment fund is then compared with the no-commission universal life policy's cash value at various intervals.

In Chapter Nine, John, our theoretical primary family income earner, decided that his budget couldn't afford the higher annual premiums of a no-commission universal life policy. There was no need for him to consider the relative value between no-commission term and no-commission universal life. His first and most important goal was to purchase the amount of life insurance he needed, as calculated in Chapter Eight, at a premium rate his budget could afford.

Let's change this scenario and say that John can afford the higher no-commission universal life annual premium. His next step therefore, is to compare the relative value of buying no-commission term insurance with that of no-commission universal life.

Certain professionals, CPAs and stockbrokers primarily, have been saying for years to buy term insurance and invest the difference between the term and permanent insurance premium. They argue that this invested "side fund" will far exceed the permanent insurance cash value. This was true before the arrival of no-commission universal life. However, with its availability the results of this buy-term-and-invest-the- difference strategy are no longer favorable.

Mark Twain once said that there are "lies, damn lies and statistics." When comparing the relative value of buying term and investing the difference versus a no-commission universal life policy's cash value one key assumption will dictate the results. This assumption is the amount of assumed interest this theoretical buy-term-and-invest-the-difference side fund will earn. If the net aftertax assumed interest earned on this side fund is at least 10%, the results are decidedly in favor of buying term and investing the difference.

It is, however, my professional opinion that using such a high assumed net aftertax interest rate will not produce a fair comparison. The investment component of life insurance, its cash value, should be considered part of your most conservative category of investments. Therefore, it should be compared to an equally conservative investing of a theoretical buy-term- and-invest-the-difference side fund.

Exhibit 10-1, on page 81, is a comparison between a no-commission five-year level term policy and a no-commission universal life policy for John. The no-commission universal life policy is based on endowment at age 95 using an interest credited assumption of 8.5%. The theoretical buy-term-and-invest-the-difference side fund is assumed to earn 9.5%. The no-commission policy has a significant advantage because its cash value grows tax- deferred, while the side fund is fully taxable. Assuming a 30% marginal tax rate for this comparison, the net interest rate for the theoretical side fund is 6.65%.

I used a financial calculator to make this comparison. I entered the difference between the no-commission term premium and the no-commission universal life premium as a payment, entered the side fund net interest rate of 6.65%, entered the period of time being considered and then requested the future value.

Exhibit 10-1 presents the buy-term-and-invest-the-difference strategy versus the no-commission universal life cash value for John, a 38-year-old non-smoker in good health for $600,000:

EXHIBIT 10-1

Age	No-Commission Universal Life Annual Premium	Five-Year Level Annual Term Premium	Accumulated Difference @ 6.65%	No-Commission Universal Life Cash Value
38	$2,623	$702	$2,049	$2,280
39	"	"	4,234	4,383
40	"	"	6,564	6,421
41	"	"	9,050	8,420
42	"	"	11,701	10,343
		2nd five-year premium		
47	"	965*	26,243	23,455
		3rd five-year premium		
52	"	1,547*	42,762	44,420
		4th five-year premium		
57	"	2,699*	58,538	71,934

* The projected premiums for the second, third and fourth five-year periods were obtained from a proposal illustration sent by Ameritas. This information isn't available from the charts in Appendix E.

If the surrender value (which is the value of the policy if it is canceled) is being compared, the no-commission universal life policy's cash value will be included in John's income and subject to income taxes, to the extent it exceeds the cumulative premiums paid. Therefore, the 15-year and 20-year cash values must be presented as their aftertax values. (There is no taxable gain until the 13th year, when the cash value exceeds the cumulative premiums paid). Assuming a 30% tax rate, the aftertax surrender values of the no-commission universal life policy in this example is $42,898 in 15 years and $66,092 in 20 years. These aftertax amounts are in contrast to the accumulated side fund of $42,762 in 15 years and $58,538 in 20 years, which are already expressed as aftertax amounts.

Those who are exceptionally astute may notice that if John had the bad judgment to die, the buy-term-and-invest-the-difference scenario would be a better buy since the side fund is in addition to the death benefit of $600,000, while the no-commission universal life policy's death benefit of $600,000 includes the cash value. And you are right. If this is a concern for you the no-commission universal life policy can be purchased with an increasing death benefit. Using this strategy, the annual target premium is higher, the cash value is higher and the death benefit is the sum of the initial death benefit ($600,000) plus the policy cash value.

Exhibit 10-2, on page 83, compares our no-commission five-year level term policy to a no-commission universal life policy with an increasing death benefit. The design of the no-commission universal life policy demonstrated in Exhibit 10-2 is based on accumulating a cash value of $600,000 and a death benefit of $1.2 million at age 95. That is, the death benefit is $600,000 plus the cash value. The projected annual target premium needed to attain these values is $3,616 based on current cost of insurance rates and an interest credited rate of 8.5%. This comparison is again made for a 38-year-old male non-smoker in good health.

Remember that the no-commission universal life policy's death benefit illustrated in Exhibit 10-2 is $600,000 plus the cash value. For example, the death benefit in the fifth year is $616,648.

The aftertax surrender values (assuming a 30% tax rate) for the no-commission universal life policy illustrated in Exhibit 10-

EXHIBIT 10-2

Age	No-Commission Universal Life Annual Premium	Five-Year Level Annual Term Premium	Accumulated Difference @ 6.65%	No-Commission Universal Life Cash Value
38	$3,616	$702	$3,108	$3,355
39	"	"	6,422	6,620
40	"	"	9,957	9,912
41	"	"	13,727	13,266
42	"	"	17,748	16,648
		2nd five-year premium		
47	"	965*	40,634	39,280
		3rd five-year premium		
52	"	1,547*	68,666	75,072
		4th five-year premium		
57	"	2,699*	100,328	124,453

* The projected premiums for the second, third and fourth five-year periods were obtained from a proposal illustration sent by Ameritas. This information isn't available from the charts in this book.

2 are $68,822 in 15 years and $108,871 in 20 years. These figures are in contrast to the accumulated side fund figures of $68,666 after 15 years and $100,328 after 20 years, which are already expressed as aftertax amounts.

Based on my interest credited assumptions, the no-commission universal life proposal illustration has better values. However, the differences are relatively small, especially in the first five years. Therefore, I conclude that there is no outstanding economic advantage to either buying no-commission term insurance and investing the difference between its premium and the premium for a no-commission universal life policy or buying a no-commission universal life policy.

To put the tremendous advantages of no-commission universal life policies versus full-commission permanent policies in perspective, Exhibit 10-3 presents a comparison of a full-commission universal life policy with buying term and investing the difference. This is based on the same no-commission five- year level term policy used in Exhibits 10-1 and 10-2 and the agent-sold, full-commission universal life policy that was used in Exhibit 7-2. The full-commission universal life illustration is based on an interest credited rate of 8.5% and current cost of insurance assumptions. Exhibit 10-3 demonstrates this comparison for a 38-year-old male non-smoker in good health with a death benefit of $600,000:

EXHIBIT 10-3

Age	No-Commission Universal Life Annual Premium	Five-Year Level Annual Term Premium	Accumulated Difference @ 6.65%	No-Commission Universal Life Cash Value
38	$5,920	$702	$5,566	0
39	3,150	"	8,548	0
40	"	"	11,728	4,958
41	"	"	15,120	7,570
42	"	"	18,737	10,335
		2nd five-year premium		
47	"	965*	39,161	26,519
		3rd five-year premium		
52	"	1,547*	63,796	46,836
		4th five-year premium		
57	"	2,699*	90,770	71,934

* The projected premiums for the second, third and fourth five-year periods were obtained from a proposal illustration sent by Ameritas. This information isn't available from the charts in Appendix E.

As you can see, the argument to buy term and invest the difference has some real merit if your only permanent insurance option were to buy a full-commission policy. This is especially true during the first five years when the cash value of the typical full-commission policy is very low due to the amortization of the very high first-year commissions.

The decision to purchase no-commission term insurance or no-commission universal life for family protection life insurance is first made based on the family's cash flow. If the higher no-commission universal life annual premium is just not possible, then the decision is simple. However, if your budget can accommodate the higher annual premium you can chose between the no-commission term and universal life policies.

If you are right on top of your finances and would actually invest the savings between the term and no-commission universal life premiums, and if you are certain that your life insurance needs will end in 20 years or so, it may make more sense to purchase a no-commission term insurance policy from either Ameritas or USAA.

On the other hand, if you are like most people and would likely spend the premium difference on consumer enjoyment, then no- commission universal life is probably a better choice.

Finally, you should recognize that the no-commission universal life policy gives you more flexibility if you ultimately decide to continue the life insurance at its initial death benefit amount or at a reduced amount until it matures, which is a nice way of saying until you die. The no-commission five-year level term policy used for our comparison has projected premiums for each five-year period until John reaches 82 years of age as shown in Exhibit 10-4 on page 86.

This escalation of premiums is the essence of term insurance. These much higher projected premium rates will come due when you are retired and have reduced income. Continuing term insurance until life expectancy and beyond will become too expensive and the term insurance policy will ultimately be canceled.

If the no-commission universal life policy was purchased and in later years the life insurance is no longer necessary, you may cancel the policy for its cash value, less any taxes due. The projected aftertax value of the no-commission universal life policy used in Exhibit 10-1 is $106,879 at age 65, assuming a 30%

EXHIBIT 10-4

Death Benefit: $600,000
Ameritas No-Commission Five-Year Level Term

Ages	Projected Five-Year Level Annual Premium
58 to 62	$4,691*
63 to 67	8,207*
68 to 72	14,051*
73 to 77	23,429*
78 to 82	39,191*

* The projected premiums for these five-year periods were obtained from a proposal illustration sent by Ameritas. This information isn't available from the charts in Appendix E.

income tax bracket. If you decided to continue the full amount of life insurance, the projected annual premium would continue to be $2,623. Or the original policy for $600,000 could be decreased to an amount desired, and it would be possible to withdraw a significant amount of cash value and pay no future premiums. This considerable flexibility is demonstrated in Exhibit 11-3 on page 93.

There is really no outstanding economic advantage for buying term and investing the difference over buying no-commission universal life. I have done hundreds of these calculations for my clients and they have always come out similar to the comparisons done in Exhibits 10-1 and 10-2. If your budget can handle the higher no-commission universal life premiums, your decision should be made on the more subjective factor of whether the greater flexibility inherent with the no-commission universal life policy is important for you. And as you will see in Chapter Eleven, no-commission universal life policies have some interesting investment characteristics as well.

CHAPTER ELEVEN

INVESTMENT CHARACTERISTICS OF NO-COMMISSION UNIVERSAL LIFE

As stated earlier, I believe permanent life insurance should not be considered an investment, but rather primarily a risk management asset. I have also asserted that there are only three principal reasons for the purchase of life insurance.

Unfortunately, this opinion isn't shared by the life insurance industry and its agents. I have seen many exotic schemes for selling permanent life insurance primarily for its investment characteristics. Buying life insurance primarily as an investment is not a good idea. (See Appendix G. If you are interested in reading about an example of an inappropriate way of using life insurance as an investment, do so now and then return to this chapter.)

Agent-sold, full-commission life insurance has two costs associated with it that don't apply to conventional investments, such as a mutual fund. The first cost is the very high policy distribution costs of 110% to 125% of the first-year premium with subsequent policy expenses of 5% to 20% for another four to nine years. Even with a load mutual fund, the commission rate is generally only 4% to 8% of the amount invested.

The other cost associated with life insurance is the expense of providing the death benefit. If life insurance is bought for investment purposes, the death benefit isn't objectively required. Therefore, the cost of providing an unnecessary death benefit will detract substantially from the investment return.

These two costs make life insurance purchased for its investment characteristics simply not competitive with a conventional investment, such as a mutual fund.

Life insurance should only be purchased for risk management purposes (with one exception that is explained in Chapter Twelve). By far the most frequent reason for the purchase of life insurance is to protect the family from the unexpected death of the primary family income earner. There are however, under current tax law, certain tax advantages associated with life insurance policies that shouldn't be ignored. Therefore, using a no-commission universal life policy, purchased for family protection reasons, for certain investment needs is a prudent step to consider.

Essentially, with a no-commission universal life policy the annual premium is debited with the cost of insurance and policy expenses (like having a term insurance policy within the no-commission universal life policy) and the remaining premium earns interest tax-deferred at the current credited rate. The cash value can be withdrawn on a first in, first out (FIFO) basis for income tax purposes if certain premium amount restrictions are met. That is, cash value can be withdrawn from the policy tax-free until the withdrawals exceed the amount of cumulative premiums paid into the policy. But, it should be noted that such withdrawals reduce the policy death benefit on a dollar-for-dollar basis.

Using a universal life policy purchased for family protection for the dual purpose of also providing an investment vehicle is only relevant if you are purchasing a no-commission universal life policy because its very low policy acquisition expenses allow for an immediate, and much stronger, cash value compared to a full-commission permanent policy.

John, our theoretical primary family income earner from previous chapters, was considering the purchase of a no- commission universal life policy in which the annual target premium was $2,623. The projected cash value for this policy in five years (see Exhibit 7-1) is $10,343. John could withdraw $5,000, for example, on a tax-free basis under current tax law at the end of the fifth year. This would reduce the original death benefit of

$600,000 to $595,000. Such an unplanned withdrawal would affect the original goal of endowing the policy at age 95 (policy cash value and death benefit are approximately equal at age 95, which is the definition of a permanent policy). To re-establish this endow-at-95 goal would require a recalculation of the annual target premium. In this instance, the unplanned withdrawal was made for an unexpected emergency purpose.

No-commission universal life can serve the dual function of providing family protection and funding an anticipated need for cash. For example John, in addition to requiring a life insurance policy for family protection needs, also wishes to invest $10,000, which may be needed at any time in the next two or three years. (John may be promoted, requiring a move to an area with higher home prices. John will then need the $10,000 as an additional down payment for a new home). In other words, at the time the no-commission universal life policy is purchased by John, he already anticipates the need for cash in two or three years. He can therefore structure his purchase of the no-commission universal life policy to include a planned withdrawal of a portion of the policy cash value.

If John were my client, I might recommend that he add $10,000 to the annual target premium the first year. I would calculate the value of $10,000 earning 8.5% (the assumed interest credited rate for the no-commission universal life policy) in three years. This comes to approximately $12,775, rounded off to $13,000. Then I would program into the proposal illustration for John's no-commission universal life policy this additional premium of $10,000 in the first year, a withdrawal in three years of $13,000 and an initial death benefit of $613,000. The death benefit is increased because withdrawal of $13,000 will reduce the policy death benefit by that amount. The computer searches for the annual target premium needed to endow the policy at age 95, taking into consideration the other requirements factored into the proposal. The revised annual target premium is $2,641, with the additional deposit of $10,000 the first year. Exhibit 11-1 is

John's proposal illustration for a no-commission universal life policy that serves the dual purpose of providing family protection and a vehicle for his specific investment need.

EXHIBIT 11-1

AMERITAS NO-COMMISSION UNIVERSAL LIFE

Death Benefit: $613,000   Age: 38 Male

Interest Credited Assumption: 8.5%   Non-Smoker

Age	Annual Premium	Investment Deposit	Withdrawls	Cash Value	Death Benefit
38	$2,641	$10,000	0	$13,146	$613,000
39	"	0	0	16,189	"
40	"	0	0	19,248	"
41	"	0	$13,000	8,224	600,000
95	"	0	0	600,000	606,000

The additional deposit, or premium, in the first year of $10,000 is illustrated to earn interest at the assumed interest credited rate, which in this exhibit is 8.5%. The withdrawal of $13,000 at the beginning of the fourth year is tax free because it does not exceed the cumulative premiums paid. The $13,000 withdrawal reduces the cash value and the death benefit. Note that this additional deposit and withdrawal doesn't affect the life insurance goal of buying a policy for $600,000 that will endow at age 95.

Another example of using a no-commission universal life policy for the dual purpose of providing family protection and providing an appropriate investment vehicle is funding for a child's college education.

John would like to fund his 10-year-old son's college education. Based on today's cost, John believes he will need $4,000 a year for four years, beginning eight years from now. We can assume that college costs will increase 5% annually. Therefore, John will need approximately $6,000 for his son's first year of college, $6,200 for the second year, $6,500 the third year and $6,800 the final year. The present value of $6,000 in eight years assuming 8.5% interest is approximately $3,100; for $6,200, the present value is $3,230; for $6,500, the present value is $3,380; and for $6,800, the present value is $3,540. If John invests $3,100 the first year, $3,230 the second year, $3,380 the third year, and $3,540 the fourth year, in addition to the annual target premium needed to endow his no-commission universal life policy at age 95, he will be able to withdraw the amounts calculated when needed. Because he will be withdrawing a cumulative total of $25,500, the no-commission universal life proposal illustration will be programmed to have an initial death benefit of $625,500 in order to retain a death benefit of $600,000 after the withdrawals.

Exhibit 11-2 is John's proposal illustration for a no- commission universal life policy with the planned educational funding

EXHIBIT 11-2

AMERITAS NO-COMMISSION UNIVERSAL LIFE

Death Benefit: $625,500   Age: 38 Male
Interest Credited Assumption: 8.5%   Non-Smoker

Age	Annual Premium	Investment Deposit	Withdrawls	Cash Value	Death Benefit
38	$2,641	$3,100	0	$5,643	$625,500
39	"	3,230	0	11,528	"
40	"	3,380	0	17,832	"
41	"	3,540	0	24,639	"
42	"	0	0	27,936	"
47	"	0	$6,000	37,921	619,500
48	"	0	6,200	36,326	613,300
49	"	0	6,500	34,146	606,800
50	"	0	6,800	31,308	600,000
95	"	0	0	600,000	606,000

investment.

As was the case in the example presented in Exhibit 11-1, the withdrawals are tax free because they don't exceed the cumulative premiums paid.

The strategy of using a no-commission universal life policy purchased for family protection needs as an investment vehicle places the horse before the cart. That is, the primary reason for purchasing the no-commission universal life policy is to provide family protection. However as an adjunct, this policy can also serve the purpose of accumulating cash on a tax- deferred basis, which can be withdrawn tax free until the withdrawals equal the cumulative premiums paid.

These strategies are successful as long as the tax code allows the tax-free withdrawal of cash value until it equals premiums paid. If the tax laws change so that any withdrawals are subject to taxation on an interest earned first basis, this dual investment strategy would no longer be appropriate. In this case, John would be faced with having to recognize the withdrawals in our examples as income.

Even if there is no specific investment need that can be blended in with the permanent life insurance purchase, the need for family protection life insurance will presumably lessen as the children grow up and other assets are accumulated to provide such protection. Ultimately, there may no longer be the need for life insurance at all. At such a time the no- commission universal life policy could be surrendered for its cash value. Again using John as our example, the no-commission universal life policy for $600,000 would have a gross cash value when John is 65 of approximately $122,000. If John surrendered the policy at age 65, the projected aftertax policy value would be approximately $107,000, assuming a 30% income tax bracket. Under these circumstances, the no-commission universal life policy acts like a forced savings plan.

Or John may decide that his life insurance need at age 65 is only $100,000. He could reduce his policy death benefit to $100,000 at age 65, withdraw approximately $93,000 of his cash value and have no more projected premiums. John would include in his income the value of the withdrawals in excess of the cumulative premiums he has paid. In this situation, he has paid cumulative premiums of $70,821, and therefore will include $22,179 ($93,000 - $70,821) as income. In a 30% tax bracket, the aftertax value of John's withdrawal is $86,346. Exhibit 11-3 demonstrates this scenario:

EXHIBIT 11-3			
AMERITAS NO-COMMISSION UNIVERSAL LIFE			
Death Benefit: $600,000			Age: 38 Male
Interest Credited Assumption: 8.5%			Non-Smoker
Age	Annual Premium	Cash Value	Death Benefit
38	$2,623	$ 2,280	$600,000
42	"	10,340	"
47	"	23,455	"
52	"	44,470	"
65	-93,000 (withdrawl)	119,249	100,000
70	0	30,684	100,000
75	0	39,261	"
95	0	114,377	115,521

Buying no-commission universal life because it is a forced savings plan seems a weak argument until you consider that the cash value will be approximately equal to a strategy of investing the difference between the no-commission universal life and the term insurance annual premiums as was demonstrated in Chapter Ten.

No-commission universal life purchased for family protection purposes can provide an appropriate investment vehicle given the right circumstances. In our examples, investing in his no- commission universal life policy was a good option for John because his investment earnings were tax free under current tax law. And even if there are no specific investment requirements, the purchase of a no-commission universal life policy can provide you with a nice retirement fund.

I don't advise that you try to set up a dual insurance and investment program on your own. As the saying goes, a little knowledge can be a dangerous thing. Retaining a fee-for-service life insurance adviser is ideal for this type of situation.

The next two chapters discuss the two other major reasons to buy life insurance.

Chapter Twelve

Life Insurance as an Estate Planning Asset

This chapter is a brief discussion of life insurance purchased as an estate planning asset, which is the second of three major reasons to buy life insurance. The final reason to purchase life insurance, to fund obligations associated with the transfer of closely-held businesses, is discussed in Chapter Thirteen.

There are three phases to our financial lives: accumulation of wealth, conservation of wealth, and distribution of wealth.

Family protection life insurance, discussed in Chapter Eight, is generally required during the accumulation phase. During this accumulation phase, the family protection requirement for life insurance is to provide sufficient capital to satisfy your survivor's income goal. Therefore, if you have the bad judgment to die, your life insurance is your primary estate asset.

The most common approach to assigning life insurance proceeds, as mentioned in Chapter Eight, is to have your spouse as beneficiary with children as contingent beneficiaries. However, a prudent individual may wish to do some life insurance estate planning, which is a more sophisticated approach to the management of your life insurance proceeds.

Let's again use our theoretical primary family income earner, John, who has purchased a $600,000 life insurance policy and has an estate of $793,000 including life insurance, but not including the house and personal property. (This figure is taken from the worksheet in Chapter Eight.) There are three major problem scenarios with naming his wife as the primary beneficiary and children as contingent beneficiaries of his life insurance:

1. If his spouse died first or they died together, his children would be entitled to their share of the insurance proceeds at their age of majority, which in most states is 18. If there were two children, each would receive a six-figure amount at a very immature age. The possible result is COKE AND CORVETTES.

2. John's wife receives his life insurance proceeds directly. She then remarries. Five years later she dies and state law requires that half of her estate, including the life insurance proceeds, must go to the second husband. Or 10 years later they divorce and in settlement he receives half of her assets, which would include the life insurance proceeds.

3. John's wife is a spendthrift and naive about investments. Within five years she has dissipated half of the insurance proceeds.

There is a very simple solution to all of these problems - retain an estate planning attorney (how to find one is explained later in this chapter) to draft a self-trusteed revocable trust. This trust becomes the beneficiary of the life insurance. The benefits of a trust are, among other things:

1. If both parents are gone, the children are provided for from the trust fund. Principal distributions from the trust can be delayed until the children are older and predictably more mature. For example, principal distributions could be delayed so that one-third of the principal is distributed at ages 25, 30 and 35.

2. The trust can have what is known as a QTIP provision, which provides that all the income is paid to John's wife, but principal is given to her only as needed. And under no circumstances can the principal be given to her second husband.

3. The trustee, which could be a bank trust department, will prudently invest the funds for the family's benefit.

After all, if you are committed to planning you might as well do it right. This additional step will provide prudent "people planning" to work in conjunction with your family financial protection planning. Finding an expert estate planning attorney to execute appropriate estate planning documents is strongly recommended.

While many of us strive to succeed in the difficult arena of the competitive marketplace, once we have there are new sets of problems. Individuals with net worths in excess of $600,000 and couples with net worths in excess of $1.2 million face the onerous federal estate tax. (Couples without proper estate planning could unnecessarily expose estate assets to the estate tax with estates over $600,000).

The federal estate and gift tax is an excise tax levied on the value of assets transferred either by gift or at death.

Over the years I have been amazed at how many wealthy people pay very little attention to their estate planning. I am sure that many reading this book have either inadequate or very flawed estate planning. This will result in the U.S. Treasury receiving a far greater amount of your estate than is necessary. There are some very basic tax planning steps that can save tremendous sums.

The estate planning I do typically results in potential estate tax savings of $100,000 to $500,000 for the client, so this issue isn't of esoteric interest to a few billionaires.

I would love to dazzle you with my estate planning creativity and acumen but it wouldn't accomplish very much because estate planning is very complicated and would require an entire book to cover the various aspects in the kind of detail necessary to adequately communicate their subtleties. Estate planning is not like a puzzle, where one piece adds to the total picture. It is more like chess, in which one moves creates multiple changes.

The best advice I can give wealthy readers, for now, is to locate an attorney who is an expert in estate planning. The most efficient way to do this is to contact several bank trust departments and ask their trust officers for the name of an attorney who does the best estate planning in your area. If you live in a small or medium-sized city, you should probably contact bank trust departments in a large metropolitan area. Estate planning is a legal specialty that isn't usually found in smaller communities.

Bank trust officers are like operating room nurses. They know which attorneys (surgeons) are adept at estate planning. And frequently bank trust officers are a valuable addition to your estate planning team.

Locating an expert estate planning attorney is critical. It has been my experience that attorneys who don't specialize in estate planning don't have the necessary knowledge or training to provide the kind of advice and documents that are necessary to minimize exposure to the estate tax and maximize creative "people planning" ideas.

The other useful estate planning information I can share is to discuss here the primary needs for life insurance as an estate planning asset.

There are three basic needs for estate planning life insurance. Life insurance can be purchased to provide the necessary liquidity to pay the federal estate tax, which will be roughly 50% of the value of assets in excess of $600,000 for individuals and $1.2 million for couples. Liquidity may be needed particularly for estates that have hard-to-market assets, such as real estate, or assets that should be retained, such as a closely-held business.

With certain exceptions, the federal estate tax is due in nine months after death. Without proper planning, the requirement to pay this tax could cause the forced sale or liquidation of hard-to-market assets, which could result in a substantial loss of their true market values. Or the requirement to pay the federal estate tax could result in the sale of assets you may have wanted retained.

The purchase of life insurance to cover all or a portion of these anticipated federal estate taxes can prevent the forced sale of hard-to-market assets at a loss.

Rather than the insurance being used to protect your family directly, it protects your accumulated wealth from a forced sale. In almost every estate liquidity need, permanent life insurance should be purchased. Term insurance is inappropriate because the insurance must remain in force until death and term insurance premiums become too costly when you approach life expectancy. Exhibit 10-4, demonstrates the extraordinarily high cost of term insurance as the insured reaches life expectancy.

One key point you must keep in mind: Life insurance used to provide estate liquidity should not be subject to the estate tax. There are several planning techniques that can be used to prevent these life insurance proceeds from being taxed in your estate. The two most common methods are establishing an irrevocable trust as the owner and beneficiary and having adult children own and be the beneficiaries of your life insurance. The estate-tax-free nature of the life insurance proceeds under these methods makes it a very valuable estate planning asset.

With either of these approaches, the life insurance proceeds aren't used to pay the estate taxes directly. Rather, the proceeds are used to purchase estate assets at their fair market values, or to loan cash to the estate. Either way, the estate has the needed cash to pay the estate settlement costs, including estate taxes.

The second major use of estate planning life insurance is to provide estate equalization between your heirs. For example, if you own a closely-held business in which some, but not all, of your children are active participants, it would be unwise to plan for the distribution of your estate in a manner that would result in active and non-active children alike inheriting an equal interest. Such a distribution would dramatically increase the likelihood that your children would become involved in disputes over the operation of the closely-held business. Children not active in the business may demand that dividends be paid, or protest that salaries paid to active participants in the business are excessive. And there may not be sufficient capital to allow for the purchase of the non- active family member's interest. Such a distribution of a closely-held family business raises the potential that future intra-family relations may be the basis of the next popular prime time soap opera.

A much better solution is to plan for children active in the business to take it over while the non-active children receive other estate assets. However, frequently the value of the business far exceeds the value of the other estate assets, making the equalization of inheritance difficult, if not impossible.

Permanent life insurance can enable you to distribute your business to children active in it and equalize the value of inheritance for the other children. The children active in the business would own an insurance policy on your life and would be obligated to buy your business with the proceeds under the terms of a buy-sell agreement. This replaces the value of your business with cash in your estate (the life insurance proceeds) making possible an equal split for all children. Also the life insurance proceeds are not included in your estate, and therefore not subject to the estate tax.

[WARNING - WARNING - WARNING - WARNING]

The material you are about to read breaks my promise to keep this book as simple as possible. I frankly couldn't figure out a simple way to describe the final reason to use life insurance in estate planning. This foray into complicated material does not entitle the holder of this book to a refund!

[WARNING - WARNING - WARNING - WARNING]

The final reason to consider the purchase of life insurance in conjunction with estate planning involves the desire by estate owners with liquid or marketable estate assets to transfer wealth to their children and grandchildren free of the federal estate and gift tax, which is a unified tax structure. That is, wealth transfers are taxed whether they are done during lifetime as gifts, or at death.

A common strategy used to transfer wealth is to take advantage of the annual gift tax exclusions. Under current law, the annual gift tax exclusion is $10,000 per year for each child and grandchild (or anyone else for that matter). For example, if the estate owners had four children and 12 grandchildren, each spouse could gift $10,000 annually to each child and grandchild for combined annual gifts of $320,000. These gifts would not be subject to the gift tax. And since the wealth has been transferred, via annual exclusion gifts, it is no longer part of the estate owners assets and therefore will not be subject to the estate tax, either.

Frequently, estate owners will gift to their children annual exclusion gifts in the form of cash that can be enjoyed any way they choose. However, the estate owners may not wish to give cash gifts to grandchildren because of their ages. Instead, gifts may be made to an irrevocable trust established by the estate owners. There are certain specific trust provisions required to achieve what is known as gifts of a present interest. A gift must be of a present interest in order for it to qualify for the annual gift tax exclusion. And there are limits on the amount of present interest annual gift exclusions to irrevocable trusts. As with other areas of estate planning, an attorney expert in this field should be used for planning advice and trust drafting.

Gifts made to the irrevocable trust, established for the grandchildren's benefit, will be invested. One of the investments that can be considered is the purchase of insurance on the life of one of the grandparents, on both their lives or on their joint lives. This purchase of life insurance isn't for risk management; the life insurance isn't needed to provide liquidity or equalize an inheritance. There isn't an objective reason for its purchase. Rather, the life insurance purchase is considered because its investment potential may be better than investing the gifts in stocks, bonds and the like.

This may seem to contradict my assertion that life insurance should not be purchased primarily as an investment. It doesn't. What was described in Chapter Eleven was life insurance purchased primarily for its investment potential based on its living benefits, or cash value. The relationship of premium payments to the policy cash value doesn't work as an investment for the reasons stated in Chapter Eleven. However, life insurance purchased as a wealth transfer asset can be appropriate as an investment because the relationship is between the premium payments and the policy death benefit. This creates a very different result.

Life insurance used as a wealth transfer asset can be appropriate because of its tax leverage. The cash value, which fuels the death benefit, grows tax deferred and the death benefit is income tax free. And when the policy is owned by and payable to a properly drafted irrevocable trust, it is also estate tax free.

To maximize the tax leverage for wealth transfer life insurance, a no-commission policy should be purchased for the obvious reason that it greatly reduces the policy's expenses. And the design of the policy should be to minimize the policy's early death benefit while maximizing the premium payments. Under this design the death benefit is the specified amount plus the policy cash value. Therefore, the death benefit will increase each year. This design produces a much better potential rate of return between the premium payments and death benefit during the period of time the insured is most likely to die.

Essentially, this design minimizes the policy's costs in the early years because the early death benefit is much lower. The cost of the life insurance policy is the company's obligation to pay a specified death benefit any time after the policy is in force. By starting with a lower death benefit, the policy's costs are lower in the early years of the policy. This allows the large premium payment to grow more rapidly, which dramatically increases the death benefit because the total death benefit is the sum of the specified amount plus the growing cash value.

Exhibit 12-1 compares a level death benefit while paying a level premium each year (shown as Design A) with minimizing the early death benefit while paying a large first-year premium (shown as Design B). The chart identifies the cumulative premiums paid, death benefit and rate of return (IRR) between premiums paid and death benefit for various years. The insured in these policy examples is a 60-year-old female who is a non-smoker in excellent health. Both designs are from the same Ameritas no-commission universal life policy:

EXHIBIT 12-1

NO-COMMISSION UNIVERSAL LIFE

Interest Credited Assumption: 8.5%

Age: 60 Female
Non-Smoker

| | Design A | | | Design B | | |
Age	Cumulative Premiums	Death Benefit	IRR	Cumulative Premiums	Death Benefit	IRR
60	$11,858	$750,000	532%	$120,000	$505,481	321%
70	113,441	"	32.9	"	597,950	17.4
75	169,876	"	15.3	"	680,174	12.2
80	226,311	"	10.4	"	785,052	9.8
85	282,746	"	6.8	"	906,347	8.4
90	339,181	"	4.7	"	1,029,481	7.4
95	396,616	"	3.3	"	1,133,293	6.6

A 60-year-old, non-smoking female in excellent health has a life expectancy of approximately 25 years, to age 85. By paying a large first-year premium and minimizing the death benefit in the early years as demonstrated in Design B, the rate of return (IRR) at age 85 and beyond is much better than that achieved with Design A. In making their decision, the estate owners must weigh the investment potential of Design B with investing in stocks, bonds, CDs, etc., also keeping in mind the risks inherent with the investment selected. And remember, insurance proceeds are income tax free.

The payment of a single large premium, or large premiums paid over several years, will cause the policy to be considered a modified endowment contract (MEC). MEC contracts are taxed on an interest earned first basis for cash value withdrawals or policy loans. In addition, if withdrawals or loans occur prior to the insured's age 59 1/2, there is a 10% penalty tax. This type of design should not be used if there is much likelihood that withdrawals or policy loans will be taken.

[End of WARNING zone - you may return to more relaxed reading.]

Unlike earlier chapters, which presented a step-by-step method for life insurance planning and purchases, the issues dealt with in this chapter are far too complicated for you to attempt it on your own. The purpose here has been only to point out potential estate planning problems or opportunities to motivate you to seek professional assistance.

Using the services of a fee-for-service life insurance adviser is particularly recommended for estate planning that requires the consideration of life insurance. The first and most important step that should be taken is the review of your existing life insurance policies. Fee-for-service life insurance advisers will be objective in their reviews of existing life insurance policies as well as in the evaluation of your need for new life insurance. And because life insurance for estate planning purposes is generally purchased in large amounts, the savings available from buying a no-commission universal life policy can be enormous. You may call the LIAA (800/521-4578) for a fee-for-service adviser referral.

CHAPTER THIRTEEN

LIFE INSURANCE AS A FUNDING ASSET FOR TRANSFERRING A BUSINESS

This chapter is for readers who own a business. Whether the business form is a corporation or partnership, your needs for business continuation planning are basically the same.

Owning a business has many rewards. Whether your business is a manufacturing operation, retail, services, etc., you know the tremendous opportunities and responsibilities inherent in such ownership. Taking a product, service or idea to the marketplace is an exciting experience. And it is a risky venture. More businesses fail than succeed.

Businesses that succeed in the marketplace are still vulnerable if proper attention isn't given to appropriate planning techniques. This chapter addresses the problems and opportunities of planning for the continuation or transfer of a business.

Business continuation planning refers to the disposition of a business interest in the event of retirement, disability or death. Generally, your business interest is the largest asset in your estate. Because most closely-held businesses are not liquid and are only marginally marketable, the unplanned disposition of a business due to disability or death is a particular risk. Some studies indicate that over 50% of closely held-businesses fail when one of the business's founders has died.

Every business owner should have a strategic plan for the disposition of his business to prevent its value from being greatly dissipated and to avoid potential conflict with a deceased or disabled partner's family. It is much better for the business disposition to be planned than for it to simply happen.

The most important step you can take is to retain an attorney with experience and knowledge in this kind of planning. If you successfully find an expert estate planning attorney, this attorney may also have expertise in business continuation planning, or a member of his firm may have the necessary background.

An example may give you an idea of the importance of business continuation planning and some of the variables that should be considered.

Two unrelated individuals have equal ownership in a manufacturing business. One of these co-owners, whom we will call Bob, has a son who has worked in the business for the past 10 years. Our business owners are both 55 years old. They haven't done any business continuation planning. Bob has a friend, named Chuck, who also owns a business. Chuck's partner recently died. Bob is aware that Chuck and his deceased partner's family have been locked in a battle. First, the partner's family wanted to help run the business, which Chuck absolutely refused to allow. Now they are fighting over the value of the partner's interest in the business. The partner's family is demanding to be bought out for a price that Chuck knows is far too high. If Chuck had to pay this price his business probably wouldn't be able to continue. Chuck advises Bob to get something in writing with his partner, Ken, before the unexpected happens.

Bob and Ken need a buy-sell agreement that plans for the transfer of business ownership in the event of permanent disability or death. Their desires for transfer of the business due to retirement will be better known in the years ahead, so there is no need to agree on this now.

The importance of a buy-sell agreement is that it sets the ground rules for the business transfer and establishes a price for this transfer. Their families, if the agreement has been drafted properly, will have to abide by the wishes they formalize in their buy-sell agreement.

Bob and Ken determine that their business is worth $2.0 million. Bob expresses the desire that his son eventually take over his interest in the business. However, Ken, at this time, does not want to be in partnership with Bob's son. Therefore, it is decided that if Bob dies or becomes totally disabled, Ken will buy Bob's business interest from his family for $1.0 million, which is Bob's share of the business.

Bob, however, sees no benefit to him of buying Ken's interest if Ken dies or becomes totally disabled since he wants his son to become a partner. So a decision is made between Ken and Bob's son that if Ken dies or becomes totally disabled, Bob's son will buy Ken's business interest for $1.0 million.

The reason Bob doesn't want to buy Ken's business interest if Ken dies or becomes totally disabled is because eventually he will pass the business on to his son. If he purchased Ken's interest for $1.0 million it would increase the value of his interest in the business to $2.0 million. Remember that the estate tax is approximately 50% of the asset value in excess of $1.2 million for couples. To plan for Bob to buy Ken's business interest and then leave it to his son would exacerbate his estate tax obligation since the value of Bob's business interest would be $2.0 million rather then $1.0 million. And if Bob had other children who didn't work in the business, it would exacerbate his estate equalization problem. I have intentionally used this slight complication to point out the interrelationship between estate and business continuation planning. In fact, this interrelationship is synergistic.

Ken has agreed to buy Bob's business interest for $1.0 million if Bob dies or becomes totally disabled and Bob's son has agreed to buy Ken's business interest for $1.0 million if Ken dies or becomes totally disabled. Where are Ken and Bob's son going to get the funds to fulfill this agreement? The fact this book is about life insurance should give you a good clue.

These agreements should be funded with life insurance and with an insurance product known as disability buy-out insurance. (The various forms of disability insurance aren't discussed in this book.) Ken would own and be beneficiary of a life insurance policy on Bob's life, as well as owning a disability buy-

out insurance policy. And Bob's son would own and be beneficiary of a life insurance policy on Ken's life, as well as owning a
disability buy-out policy.

Whether the life insurance used to fund these buy-sell
agreements should be no-commission term or no-commission
universal life would depend on the cash flow available and the
length of time Bob and Ken believe these agreements would be
necessary. Unlike estate planning life insurance, which should
be permanent insurance, there are many variables to be considered before choosing between no-commission term and no-
commission universal life for funding a buy-sell agreement.

Admittedly, there are other factors not mentioned here that
would be considered during this process. But this example
provides an understanding of the importance of a buy-sell
agreement and presents some of the important variables involved.

Not all businesses are co-owned. Many are solely owned.
Solely owned businesses are particularly exposed because there
is no co-owner to establish the planning such as described in our
example of Bob and Ken. Sole business owners also need to
consider their options for the disposition of their business in the
event of their death.

One method is to establish a buy-sell agreement with another sole business owner providing an identical service or
product. The two owners execute an agreement detailing the
price and terms for the sale. This type of agreement should be
funded with life insurance. Unfortunately, finding a good match
with another business is very difficult. Only rarely have I seen
this work. The most common opportunity for this arrangement
is with medical and dental practices.

A more common option is for the sole owner to select a key
employee who will be asked to work with the sole owner's family
to sell, liquidate or purchase the business in the event of the
owner's demise. This key employee is compensated for his
efforts to sell or liquidate the business. If the key employee

decides to purchase the business, he is given a discount equal to his compensation for these services. The sole owner records his wishes with his attorney, accountant and family. The key employee usually isn't informed until his services are needed. Without this kind of planning, the deceased owner's family will predictably waste valuable time trying to figure out what to do after an unexpected death. And during this time the employees of the business will become discouraged due to a lack of direction.

From a life insurance planning standpoint, it is probably wise to assume the lowest possible value for your solely-owned business in the event of your demise. You can use life insurance to make up the difference. That is, if your business is valued at $500,000 with you in charge, but may be liquidated for as little as $50,000 if you die, you may wish to consider purchasing an additional $450,000 of life insurance. This additional life insurance purchase is especially relevant if you have used the full value of your business for your family protection calculations. If upon your unexpected demise your key employee is able to sell your business for much more than the $50,000, the life insurance proceeds of $450,000 will provide your family with better support than you had planned.

Regarding retirement, the sole owner should begin evaluating his employees to determine which one would have the best chance of succeeding him. Several years before retirement, the owner should formally begin grooming this employee to take over the business and purchase it at retirement. If this prospective retirement planning isn't done, the sole owner may realize that his business has little value as a retirement asset, or he may be forced to work much longer than desired.

I offer the same admonition stated in the last chapter. Business continuation planning is too complex for business owners to try on their own. You will need professional assistance from an attorney, perhaps your accountant to aid in the valuation of your business, and of course an insurance professional. The benefits of fee-for-service life insurance advisers mentioned previously apply to your business transfer life insurance needs, as well.

Chapter Fourteen

Evaluating Life Insurance Policies Presently Owned

Very few of the clients I have worked with have had much understanding of the life insurance policies they had purchased. Usually these policies are stuck in a drawer folded up like road maps. The only time they are brought out is when a life insurance agent asks to look at them.

An objective review of life insurance you already own can be very important. Regarding term insurance, you may discover that one or both of the no-commission term insurance policies from Ameritas and USAA are less expensive than the one you own. And permanent insurance should be reviewed to ascertain whether it is performing as projected when you bought it since the projections are dependent on factors that, above a minimum level, aren't guaranteed.

Evaluating term insurance is much easier than evaluating permanent insurance. If you wish to compare your term insurance policies with the no-commission term insurance offered by Ameritas and USAA, contact the insurance company you have your term insurance with and request a schedule of future premiums. Compare this schedule of premiums with the term insurance proposal illustrations from Ameritas or USAA.

Notice if premiums being projected for your current term policy are dependent on your proof of continued good health. Having to prove continued good health in order to qualify for the company's most competitive rate is referred to as a re-entry provision, which was discussed in Chapter Six and Appendix F. Remember, neither of the no-commission term insurance policies recommended in this book have this re-entry requirement.

That is, the projected future premiums don't depend on proof that you are in the same health as when the policy was originally purchased.

If either no-commission term policy from Ameritas or USAA is projected to be less expensive than the term policy you may presently own, you should consider replacing it with this lower cost alternative. The only drawback to replacing a more expensive term insurance policy with a lower priced new one is the existence of a two-year contestability and suicide period. If material misrepresentations are made on the new application or death has been by suicide, the insurance company would deny the benefit during the first two years. The term insurance policy already owned may be past the two-year period.

Evaluating and comparing permanent insurance is much more difficult because there are more components to consider.

To evaluate your permanent insurance policy, contact your insurance company and request what is generically known as an in-force ledger. Ask that this in-force ledger be run for at least 20 years into the future. (If you have difficulty getting cooperation from the insurance company, write a letter to the company's president requesting this information. I find this works very well.) This in-force ledger will show the projected and guaranteed cash value and death benefits based on your premium payment schedule.

If you have your original proposal illustration, compare it with the in-force ledger. Look especially at the difference in the cash values between the original proposal illustration and the in-force ledger. You may discover that because of changes in non-guaranteed factors, like cost of insurance rates or interest credited rates, that your policy coverage will not continue as long as originally projected. If you don't have your original proposal illustration, you will have to compare the in-force ledger with what you remember about the basic design of the policy. For example, based on the non-guaranteed factors at the time you purchased the policy, you may have anticipated that you would only have to pay premiums for, say, seven years. The in-force ledger will either confirm the soundness of this original assumption or alert you to the necessity of paying premiums for a longer period of time in order to achieve your original goal for the life insurance.

Don't be afraid to call the insurance company's policyholder services department to ask them any questions you may have.

Reviewing permanent policies purchased during the 1980s is particularly important. The 1980s saw very competitive pricing by life insurance companies. These competitive prices were based on factors that, above a minimum level, aren't guaranteed. The very high interest rates during this time have come down and so have internal policy interest credited factors. Further, some companies in their quest for premium dollars were assuming cost of insurance rates that weren't justified. Many of these companies with cost of insurance rates that were too low have had to increase them. Many owners of permanent life insurance purchased during the 1980s have policies that won't perform as they were illustrated. The danger is that these policies are underfunded and will require much larger premiums than were projected for the coverage to continue.

If you don't need your policy death benefit, you should determine whether the investment component (cash value) rate of return is reasonable relative to that of other investments available to you.

To determine this, you need to compute the internal rate of return (IRR) for the policy cash value, using a financial calculator. (Note, it is probably reasonable to use the projected cash value column rather than the guaranteed cash value column.) Enter the current year cash value as the opening balance using the present value key. Then enter the scheduled future premiums for the time period you are analyzing as payments. Then enter the cash value in the year ending the period of analysis as a negative payment and hit the IRR key. This will tell you the internal rate of return for the projected cash value. (Refer to your financial calculator's manual for instructions on computing internal rate of return.)

While you may find that this internal rate of return is irritatingly low, for many mutual insurance companies the internal rate of return for the cash value of older policies can be amazingly strong. And remember that the cash value increases on a tax-deferred basis. If the cash value internal rate of return is reasonable, then you could decide to retain the policy. On the other hand, if the cash value internal rate of return is lower than the aftertax return on an alternative investment and the death benefit is not necessary, it might make sense to surrender the policy and invest the cash value elsewhere.

Keep in mind that if the policy is surrendered, the cash value in excess of cumulative premiums paid is considered income to you and is fully taxable. One strategy you may use to avoid including these excess premiums in income from a surrendered policy is to transfer them to a single-premium deferred annuity (SPDA). If this is done properly you will not recognize any income. This is known as a 1035 exchange. The number 1035 refers to the tax code section that allows this tax-free exchange between a life insurance policy and a SPDA. But don't use this 1035 exchange option unless the purchase of a SPDA is, in the first instance, an appropriate investment for you. One major drawback of a SPDA is that any taxable withdrawals or surrenders prior to age 59 1/2 are subject to a 10% penalty tax.

If you want to compare your permanent insurance to a proposed new policy, evaluation becomes a lot more complicated. In fact, after several attempts to write instructions for comparing an existing permanent policy with a new one, I gave up. There are simply too many subtle variables that have to be taken into account. If this policy comparison issue comes up, you will need the assistance of a fee-for-service life insurance adviser if you want an objective and independent analysis. Or, you can send your proposal illustrations to The Beacon Co. along with $95 for each illustration you want reviewed. This review will indicate whether the illustrations suggest that the policy is overpriced, underpriced or reasonably priced. I am the president of The Beacon Co., whose address is 2822 Bay Drive, W. Bloomfield, MI 48324.

There are other reasons to consider evaluating existing life insurance. Life insurance is a complicated asset from a tax standpoint. If the insured, owner, and beneficiary of the policy have not been set up properly there can be dire tax consequences. This is particularly true of life insurance owned by wealthy individuals and business owners. I frequently see situations in which life insurance proceeds are unnecessarily exposed to the estate tax due to an agent's incompetence; even worse is when the proceeds are exposed to income taxes, which is totally unacceptable.

Even when the technical aspects of the life insurance contract were originally set up properly, new tax laws have left some pre-existing life insurance exposed to taxation. The best example of this is corporate-owned life insurance that may now be taxed under the corporate alternative minimum tax.

You don't need to leave your life insurance policies folded up in a drawer. You can and should begin a review of these policies. Whether you need to use a fee-for-service life insurance adviser to help you with this review depends on the value of the policies being reviewed and your confidence in understanding the information you are reviewing.

CHAPTER FIFTEEN

MISCELLANEOUS COMMENTS

I approach this chapter with reluctance. In earlier chapters I have attempted to go in a straight line to define how to determine the amount of life insurance you may need for family protection and how to judge whether no-commission term or no-commission universal life is most appropriate for you. I have tried to keep these discussions as simple as possible. If you are to take control of your life insurance planning you must feel confident that you understand the issues. Therefore, to provide a comprehensive discussion of other forms of term and permanent insurance is at best irrelevant to the purposes of this book and, at worst, could lead to confusion on your part. Nevertheless, there are several specific points I would like to share with you about important life insurance issues.

This book has focused on three major reasons to buy life insurance: for family protection, as an estate planning asset, and to fund obligations associated with the transfer of closely-held businesses. All three of these reasons assume that this life insurance will be needed for an extended period of time. There are, however situations in which life insurance is needed only for a short period of time. For example, you may be required by a creditor to have life insurance to cover a debt obligation. If you need life insurance for a short period of time you should consider purchasing a no-commission seven-year term policy from USAA.

The no-commission seven-year term policy offered by USAA has very low premiums for the seven-year period. However, unlike the other no-commission term policies discussed in this book, the seven-year term policy cannot be renewed after the seven- year period. After the seven-year period, you would have to apply for another no-commission seven-year term policy and satisfy the medical requirements again, if the life insurance is still needed. This policy cannot be exchanged for USAA's no-commission universal life policy. The premium rates for this no-commission seven-year term policy are listed in Appendix E.

Don't confuse the USAA no-commission seven-year term policy with the five-year level no-commission term policy sold by Ameritas. The no-commission seven-year term policy has projected premiums that go up each year for the seven-year period. With the Ameritas five-year level no-commission term policy, the premiums remain level.

If you need life insurance for an extended period of time, stick with the no-commission five-year level term offered by Ameritas or the annual renewal term offered by USAA. While it might be tempting to buy the less expensive no-commission seven-year term insurance policy, such a decision would be disastrous if your health were to fail and you couldn't buy a new policy to replace the it at the end of the seven-year period.

*   *   *   *   *   *   *   *   *   *

If I somehow haven't convinced you of the merits of buying no- commission universal life on a direct basis and you are in the market for a full-commission permanent policy, you should be cautious in your selection of a life insurance company. During the spring of 1991 four life insurance companies were seized by state insurance commissions and another half a dozen, or so, have been reported to be experiencing financial difficulties.

Determining if a life insurance company has a strong financial base is difficult for three reasons. First, most readers will not be capable of doing an independent evaluation. It's hard to know which financial parameters are important, and even knowing the important parameters, analyzing them takes expert knowledge and experience. Secondly, rating services that have historically been relied upon failed to give some companies low ratings prior to their difficulties, which kept consumers from being warned about potential danger. For example, A.M. Best, the rating service with the highest visibility, gave Executive Life of California, which was seized by the California Insurance Department in April 1991, their highest rating as late as January 1990. But they weren't alone. Standard and Poor's also gave Executive Life a strong rating, also as late as January 1990. Finally, consumers won't get much help from life insurance salesmen concerning the financial strength of companies whose policies they are recommending. Agents are rewarded for selling policies, not for providing such information.

Fortunately, after the storm comes new light. Life insurance company rating services have learned a painful lesson from failing to give low ratings to such companies as Executive Life and First Capital in time to warn consumers of impending problems. It is very likely that rating services will make adjustments in how they perform their analysis and will become more conservative. At least in the short term their ratings may become a more reliable indicator of life insurance company financial strength.

A three-year-old rating service of life insurance companies, Weiss Research, Inc., has an enviable record during this time of life insurance company difficulties. With the exception of Equitable, which they rated C+ (Best had rated them A+), Weiss had rated every company that has experienced significant financial difficulties below average or poor in 1990. Weiss analyzes the insurance company's assets relative to their chances of performing well in a moderate to severe recession. While many life insurance experts, and the companies themselves, have criticized Weiss' rating methodology, Weiss' results during the spring of 1991 can't be criticized. This may be a case of Weiss being lucky to have used a 'flawed' rating system at a time when their methodology (giving high ratings to companies with the most conservative investments) was the most accurate predictor because of the particular economic times we were going through.

It may also turn out to be similar to golf experts' poor opinion of Arnold Palmer's golf swing during the early stages of what has turned out to be a magnificent career.

Checking the financial strength ratings of life insurance companies is important for consumers to do. You can contact life insurance companies and request that they send you the most current ratings they have received from rating services. Three services rate nearly all U.S. life insurance companies: A.M. Best, Standard & Poor's qualified solvency ratings and Weiss Research, Inc. In addition, three ratings services, Standard & Poor's, Moody's and Duff & Phelps, rate insurance companies for a fee. Because the insurance company must pay a fee of generally $15,000 to $30,000, not all life insurance companies will have these fee ratings.

One word of caution - the various rating services use different letter grades. Request that each rating company include a description of their rating system so that you may interpret the relative value of the rating given to the insurance company whose financial strength you are reviewing.

With the recent history of the major rating services' ineptitude, it may be worthwhile to contact Weiss Research, Inc., (800/ 299-9222) and purchase the written reports that support their letter grade for the life insurance company you are considering. The short report costs $25.00, a more detailed report costs $45.00 and a verbal report runs $9.00. As things currently stand, Weiss probably has the most conservative rating system. They may unfairly give some companies a lower rating than they deserve, but I suspect that Weiss won't rate a company higher than they deserve. It may turn out that the many experts who have criticized Weiss will be proven right. However, until the more highly regarded rating services have won back consumers' confidence (or, in this case mine), Weiss may be something of a safety net.

My advice regarding checking the financial strength of life insurance companies is to review two or three rating services' ratings and only buy from life insurance companies that have received a strong rating from each of the services you review.

* * * * * * * * * *

Permanent insurance is known as universal life, flexible premium whole life, interest-sensitive whole life, participating whole life and variable life. These various forms of permanent life insurance invariably lead to considerable confusion as agents selling one type criticize the other types. Unfortunately, criticisms made during competitive battles add little understanding for a consumer caught in the middle. For example, a common criticism directed at universal life is that it isn't guaranteed, while whole life is. This criticism is simply wrong and ignores several relevant facts. While each type of permanent insurance (including universal life) has certain guaranteed factors, all forms of permanent life insurance depend on non-guaranteed components in order to be priced competitively. The value of all permanent forms of life insurance depends on the three basic components, described in Chapter One:

1. Cost of paying death claims;
2. Expenses; and
3. Investment return on premiums held until death claims are paid.

The cost of paying death claims and the return on investments are not known in advance, therefore policy performance above specified policy guarantees will fluctuate according to each company's experience with death claims and investment results.

The differences agents describe are primarily due to semantics. For example, to be competitive, participating whole life policies depend on annual dividends paid to the policyowner, which aren't guaranteed. This is in contrast to universal life, which has current cost of insurance rates and current interest credited rates that aren't guaranteed either. The terminology is different, making it confusing for consumers and allowing agents to distort the message, but the three basic components that contribute to policy values are the same. (See Appendix H.)

Variable life, one form of permanent life insurance, is a special case. The policyowner may select from a variety of mutual funds for the "investing" of his cash value. The performance of the mutual fund selected will have a direct effect on the policy's cash value. The policyowner takes the risk associated with the mutual fund selected. In other words, there are generally no cash value guarantees with variable life policies.

In Chapter Ten, I stated that the cash value in your permanent insurance policy should be considered part of your most conservative category of investments. Purchasing variable life and selecting a stock or bond mutual fund, which subjects the principal to risk, contradicts this advice. Of course you could select a money market or fixed investment mutual fund within a variable life policy, which has no risk to principal, but this is not advisable because the expenses associated with a variable life policy are generally higher than the expenses for other forms of permanent insurance. Simply put, don't buy variable life insurance.

*   *   *   *   *   *   *   *   *   *

There is a new type of permanent life insurance, being marketed primarily to wealthy consumers for estate liquidity, that is known as a joint and survivor policy, or a second-to- die policy. This policy insures both the husband and wife and pays its death benefit at the second death. The rationale for second-to-die policies is that it is possible to delay estate taxes until the second death because estate tax provisions allow a surviving spouse to receive assets free of the estate tax. The estate tax will be payable upon the death of the surviving spouse. Most major life insurance companies have developed second-to-die policies and the competition among them to sell these policies, generally for large premiums, is fierce.

There are three significant problems with second-to-die policies. First, some insurance agents naturally gravitate to new types of policies, giving little thought to whether they are appropriate in every estate planning situation. I have seen situations in which second-to-die policies have been recommended that really required a single-life insurance approach. For example, if the father and one child are in business together while other children work elsewhere, it is probably most appropriate for the child working in his father's business to own a life insurance policy on his father's life under the terms of a buy-sell agreement. If a second-to-die policy is used (I have seen this recommended many times) and the mother survives the father, the child would not have ownership control of the business he is running until his mother's subsequent death. This could cause intra-family problems. Further, the business may not produce sufficient cash flow to support his mother. A single-life policy on the father's life would work much better.

Fierce competition for the sale of second-to-die policies creates a second problem: In order to win sales, some companies have designed proposal illustrations with pricing that may prove to be too low to cover eventual policy expenses. This could cause either much larger premiums than anticipated or a drop in the death benefit. Because of the tax leverage available with a life insurance policy (cash value grows tax deferred and death benefits are income tax free), it is unwise to underfund a policy. But with competition driving down projected pricing, underfunding may be the result.

The final problem involves splitting a second-to-die policy. Two situations could cause this to happen. One is the dissolution of the marriage between joint insureds. The other is a significant change in the estate tax laws. For example, the actual estate tax bracket spread for most estates is between 41% and 55%. Such a narrow spread dictates that the estate tax be postponed until the second death. However, if Congress increased the top tax bracket to, say, 70%, many estates might be better off paying some estate taxes at each death. Many second-to-die policies allow for the policy to be split in two, but, some of the costs associated with a policy split may be very high. Also, there could be a portability problem when an original second-to-die policy that is owned by an irrevocable trust is split.

These problems don't suggest that second-to-die policies should be avoided. They do, however, suggest that they should be used selectively - not as the solution to every estate liquidity problem. They have a role to play and should be used when the planning indicates that it would be in the best interest of the client.

* * * * * * * * * *

Many term insurance policies and almost all permanent insurance policies are priced on a current assumption basis. This means that while there are certain policy pricing guarantees, the decision to buy one policy over another is based on the current assumption pricing that isn't guaranteed. This fact concerns many of my clients until they realize that a policy guaranteeing its pricing has three possible outcomes, two of which aren't desirable. The insurance company may underestimate the pricing factors and will lose money on the policies. Too much of this will cause the company to become insolvent. Or, the company may overestimate the pricing factors, and the policyholder will pay too much premium for his policy. Finally, the company may estimate the pricing factors just right, which is highly unlikely.

Non-guaranteed current assumption insurance policies allow for competitive pricing since insurance companies have the flexibility to adjust the non-guaranteed factors as economic conditions change. However, some insurance companies use this non-guarantee aspect of life insurance pricing to take advantage of consumers by projecting pricing that simply is too good to be true. This is the "liar's poker" style of proposing life insurance. It is because of the problem of unreasonable proposal illustrations that I formed The Beacon Co. to provide consumers a report that tests their reasonableness. This report costs $95 per proposal illustration reviewed. The Beacon Co's. address is listed at the end of Chapter Fourteen.

Current assumption life insurance pricing makes it very important for consumers to deal with financially strong companies with a history of making realistic pricing assumptions.

*   *   *   *   *   *   *   *   *   *

In Chapters Eight, Eleven and Twelve I have described setting up the annual target premium for a no-commission universal life policy based on endowing the policy at age 95, which means that the cash value and death benefit are approximately equal when the insured reaches age 95. This is the pure definition of a permanent policy. Each exhibit assumed that the premium would be paid each year. However, no-commission universal life has such great flexibility that other premium designs can be used.

For example, you may wish to pay life insurance premiums for only a specified number of years. Our friend John may wish to limit his premium payments to the first 10 years, but still keep the endow-at-age-95 design. Exhibit 15-1 depicts an Ameritas proposal illustration with the design of endowing at age 95, but limits the projected premium payments to 10 years. Obviously, if only 10 premium payments are scheduled to be made, they must be higher than if premiums are paid each year. You will recall that the target premium, paying all years, was $2,623 for John's purchase of a $600,000 policy. (See Exhibit 7-1.) The target premium for a 38-year-old-male, non-smoker for $600,000 policy, based on current cost of insurance and an interest credited rate of 8.5% to endow the policy at 95 with only 10 premium payments is $4,343. This is demonstrated in Exhibit 15-1, on page 126.

There are two cautions associated with accelerating the premium payments. First, you must be careful to monitor the policy, as described in Chapters Seven and Fourteen, and be alert to any changes in the interest credited rate or cost of insurance

EXHIBIT 15-1

NO-COMMISSION UNIVERSAL LIFE

Death Benefit: $600,000   Age: 38 Male
Interest Credited Assumption: 8.5%   Non-Smoker

Age	Annual Premium	Cumulative Premiums Paid	Cash Value	Death Benefit
38	$4,343	$4,343	$4,167	$600,000
39	"	8,686	8,280	"
40	"	13,029	12,526	"
41	"	17,372	16,928	"
42	"	21,715	21,468	"
47	"	43,430	51,899	"
52	0	43,430	71,922	"
57	0	43,430	98,090	"
95	0	43,430	599,984	605,984

rates that would adversely affect your policy. The more acceler-
ated the premium payment schedule, the greater the impact
changes in policy interest credited rates will have.

The other caution is to keep the higher premium payments
under maximum guideline premium amounts in order to avoid
having the policy considered a modified endowment contract
(MEC). If the premium paid exceeds federal life insurance guidelines qualifying the policy as a MEC, any withdrawals of the cash
value or loans against the cash value will be taxable on an
interest-earned-first basis. And, if policy withdrawals are made
prior to age 59 1/2 they would also be subject to a 10% penalty
tax.

Nearly every life insurance company, including Ameritas
and USAA, will inform you if your planned premium design
would exceed these guidelines.

*   *   *   *   *   *   *   *   *   *

Some life insurance companies market their policies on a mass marketing basis by advertising on television or through mass mailings. While I haven't made an exhaustive study of these mass marketed policies, I do occasionally respond to their appeals to see what these companies are up to.

Every offer I have reviewed has been awful; they have been totally uncompetitive. My advice is not to buy any life insurance from these mass marketers.

Also, I have analyzed credit life insurance sold in conjunction with home mortgages or automobile financing and conclude that these policies are also very uncompetitive. In fact, the National Association of Insurance Commissioners (NAIC) initiated a probe into credit life insurance in 1991. NAIC is concerned because they believe credit life insurance, which returns only 37 cents of every premium dollar back to consumers, is uncompetitive. If you would like life insurance specifically to cover such debts, buy a no-commission term insurance policy.

PURCHASE DECISIONS

Many consumers don't seek out a life insurance agent. Generally, agents pursue potential customers. There is an old adage in the life insurance business that life insurance is sold, not bought. And because of consumer resistance to granting a soliciting agent an appointment to talk about life insurance, many agents are forced to use reasons unrelated to buying life insurance to solicit potential life insurance customers.

Currently, a popular misdirection used by life insurance agents is the practice of identifying themselves as pension administrators and consultants. In my yellow pages for the suburbs to the north of Detroit, there are approximately 50 listings for pension administrators and consultants. Of these 50, I can identify only three firms that don't sell life insurance. Many pension firms earn a substantial amount of their revenues from the sale of life insurance.

A number of years ago a client was referred to me by his attorney. This client had been working with a pension consultant to install a defined benefit pension plan for his business. The pension consultant had suggested that this client insure his pension plan. This sounded like a worthy idea and the client agreed to it. Not unlike insuring his home or autos, my client thought he was insuring the pension plan's assets. He became suspicious when he had to take a physical exam for this insurance. This suspicion led him to me. The client was told to buy permanent life insurance, which would be a pension plan asset. The amount of life insurance was $500,000 with a $12,000 annual premium. The client had no objective need for this amount of life insurance, or for the kind of insurance (permanent) being recommended.

I also had my doubts as to whether the client even needed this kind of pension plan. He was the only employee of his company, which was dependent on the financial health of the auto industry. The history of his business was several years of boom followed by several years of bust. Installing a defined benefit pension plan, which requires fixed annual contributions, is a great way to tax-defer income in the good years, but becomes an albatross during the bust years. Within two years this client had to go through the expensive process of terminating the pension plan because his business could no longer support the fixed annual pension contributions. Pension consultants who use pension design work as the camouflage to sell life insurance policies aren't very prudent in their evaluation of whether a client should even be installing a pension plan in the first place. The pension plan becomes the bait for the real action, which is to sell the life insurance.

Perhaps the all-time champion, in my experience, for attempting to mislead consumers was an idea that a firm marketing home water purification systems had. I received an invitation some time ago from such a firm requesting that area life insurance agents come to a meeting to discuss a combined marketing approach for home water purification systems and life insurance. I called this firm upon receiving my invitation, and they explained their understanding of how difficult a task it is to solicit life insurance consumers. They were offering the opportunity for interested life insurance agents to sign on with their home water purification firm and use the sale of their system for solicitation purposes. Once in the door, the life insurance agent would try to sell the prospect a home water purification system, then switch gears and try to sell life insurance as well.

Naturally, I didn't go to this meeting. But I concocted a fail-proof method for selling at least one of the products being offered. If the prospect failed to heed the dire health warnings associated with using untreated tap water and didn't purchase the home purification system, the agent would have the perfect argument for the purchase of life insurance: Most humans will die if they drink untreated tap water, therefore, the only alternative is to buy life insurance. I have wondered how many life insurance agents bought into this creative method to mislead the public.

Just before this book went to print, a gentleman did some minor maintenance work on my house. After some time I took him a cold drink and we chatted. Before long he gave me his water treatment system business card. His pitch was somewhat believable and I even ask him how much such a system would cost. Before we broke up our little chat, he announced that he was also an A.L Williams life insurance agent and could save me thousands of dollars. I believe this man is a pioneer in the two-fer opportunists club because he has sold water treatment systems for 17 years.

The solicitation method of selling life insurance will frequently result in consumers buying life insurance without a good deal of rational thought being given to that decision.

An extreme example of this non-rational consumer behavior purchasing life insurance is a client I worked with several years ago. My client at the time was 46 years old and unmarried with no children. He was adamant that he would never be married. Over a 15 year period this client had purchased 11 different whole life policies from three different insurance companies with a combined death benefit of approximately $450,000. During our meetings we determined that he had no objective need for any life insurance. So why did he buy all of these life insurance policies? His father owned a car dealership and every two years or so, one or another life insurance agent would solicit my client's father. To get rid of the agent, the father would direct the agent to his son, who would buy a small policy, with the father initially paying the premium. This apparently would satisfy the agent's desire for a commission payday, as agents repeatedly would take the small sale and leave the client's father alone for another couple of years. Not unlike an old lion, who, tired of the hunt, will be satisfied with leftover morsels that he gratefully devours before sleeping the afternoon away in the sun.

CONSUMER CONFUSION

In 1986, I was retained as a fee-for-service life insurance adviser by an area law firm to assist them in the estate planning for one of their affluent clients. This work resulted in my recommending the purchase of a $1.5 million no-commission universal life policy for estate liquidity purposes, which was purchased. In 1989 I was informed by the law firm that a life insurance agent was recommending the replacement of this no- commission universal life policy with a policy from Executive Life of California, and the law firm requested that I analyze the proposal being made. The Executive Life proposal looked, in my judgment, too good to be true. I contacted the agent and requested full disclosure of the commission and other acquisition expenses, Executive Life's investment portfolio and the assumed and guaranteed cost of insurance rates for the policy being proposed. The agent refused to provide any of this information, declaring that the commission and other expenses were not relevant, that the investment portfolio information wasn't available because of Executive Life's desire to maintain secrecy for competitive purposes (actually, the investment portfolio is available in Schedule D of each companies annual report, however, this report was dated at the time I worked with this client), and that cost of insurance information was never given out. I was able to estimate this information and informed the client of my estimates for the Executive Life policy he was being pressured to buy. The agent refuted my estimates or their importance when he felt they were damaging to his position. I warned the client that the major problem, aside from replacing a no-commission policy with a full-commission policy at his age of 70, was Executive Life's investment portfolio, which was substantially invested in below investment grade bonds (junk bonds). The agent was a much better salesman than I was an adviser and the client made, in my estimation, a very poor decision when he replaced his no- commission universal life policy with the Executive Life policy.

Early in February of 1990, First Executive Corp. announced that it was taking a $515 million charge for the fourth quarter of 1989, and that its portfolio would be worth $1.4 billion less in the market than on its books due to junk bond defaults and lower value in the market. First Executive's stock fell from a high of $17.25 in 1989 to $3.50 on February 2, 1990. From this point until April of 1991, when First Executive Corporation's insurance units were seized by state insurance bureaus, events at First Executive spiraled out of control.

In hindsight, the client realizes he should have taken my concerns about Executive Life more seriously. I am certain if insurance companies were compelled to disclose the information I suggested in Chapter Two, this client would have made a much more informed decision. But the client wanted to believe the information that the agent presented: the Executive Life policy looked so much better than his existing policy. And the agent, who I estimate earned a commission of approximately $56,000, controlled the issues to his own benefit.

In every experience I have had with a proposed Executive Life policy, the agent not only refused to disclose Executive Life's heavy investments in junk bonds, but in many instances tried to hide this fact. Clients were unfairly led to believe that Executive Life's higher projected interest rates could be achieved without greater risk.

It is unfortunate that it takes the seizure of a life insurance company for consumers to finally see through the smoke and mirrors.

Agents make many decisions concerning the sale of life insurance policies that consumers are completely unaware of.

For example, many insurance companies, including some of the most highly respected, have policies in which the agent determines the amount of commission he will earn by selecting alternative structures within the policy. (This is different from the example of the two policies with different commission rates described in Chapter Two.) Basically, the agent can offer a policy that has an investment add-on component in addition to the traditional policy cash value. The greater the investment add-on component selected by the agent, the lower the commission. And conversely, the lower (or absence of) the investment add-on component, the higher the commission. I recently reviewed a life insurance policy purchased the previous year. The commission range for both the agent and general agent was from $4,300 to $76,000. The agent selected a $76,000 commission. The client was completely unaware of this commission spread. Perhaps he was lulled into thinking the agent had his best interests in mind since she charged him a $2,500 consulting fee. Agents who select the lower commission are engaging in a form of legal rebating (rebating is discussed in Chapter Four) that life insurance state regulators either condone or don't truly understand the implications of when these policies are approved for sale in their states.

One of my all-time favorite examples of life insurance agent misbehavior is a case I was involved in several years ago. An attorney called to ask me what an intermediate bond fund with a mortality charge was. Without hesitation I told him it was a life insurance policy. The attorney was specifically told that it wasn't a life insurance policy. I was asked to contact the attorney's client, who told me the same thing. My next call, as requested by the client who by now had retained my services, was to the agent making the recommendation. He told me the same thing (an intermediate bond fund with a mortality charge). After some fancy footwork, he allowed that it was like a life insurance policy. After some more maneuvering he admitted that it was an interest-sensitive whole life policy from a large Canadian insurance company. Some weeks later we had a meeting with the agent, an attorney the agent brought along, the clients, their attorney and myself. The agent kept tying himself in knots as he attempted to extricate himself from distortion after distortion. The poor attorney who had accompanied him was as lost as his compatriot and began pounding the table and swearing. This is an old lawyer strategy: When the law is on their side, they pound the law; when the facts are on their side, they pound the facts; and when neither the law nor facts are on their side, they pound the table.

I have had many clients who have purchased insurance on the lives of their children for the stated purpose of using it to fund their children's college educations. When I point out that Jane's policy (for example), with a death benefit of $25,000, will only have a cash value of $800 when she is college age, many of these clients protest that they will use the full $25,000. Everyone needs a party pooper, and while I don't take any delight in doing it, I feel compelled to inform these poor innocents that $25,000 is the death benefit. Well, even engineers and physicians, etc., should be allowed to be stupid occasionally, it's good for balancing their other admirable traits. I have had this experience so often that I am wondering if there is a conspiracy within the life insurance industry to humiliate otherwise intelligent people.

I have frequently compared life insurance agents to magicians, and I'm a reformed magician who knows their tricks. Once you know their tricks, it is great fun watching the creative misdirections they use on their unsuspecting audience. This reminds me of my favorite card trick.

The card trick starts with me looking at the card on the bottom of the deck, shuffling the deck so that the card I have seen ends up on the top of the deck, then palming that card before handing the deck to my unsuspecting victim. I place the palmed card in my pocket as my victim vigorously shuffles the deck, which is, of course, light one card. When the shuffling is complete my victim hands me the deck, which I place in my pocket with the card I had palmed. I am able to position the palmed card at the front of the deck making it easy for me to find when needed. Let's say the card I had palmed is the six of hearts. I then ask the victim to name three suits. "Let's see, spades, hearts and clubs," my innocent friend replies. I instruct him to name two of the three he has selected. "Spades and clubs," says the dupe. I reply, "That leaves hearts. Now pick two cards in the heart suit," I instruct. "The three and 10 of hearts," my trusting counterpart says. "Pick five hearts between the three and 10," I command. "Three, four, five, six and seven," my colleague replies, feeling very much in control. "Pick three of these five heart cards," I request. "Three, four and five," my friend complies. "OK, that leaves the six and seven of hearts; pick one of them," say I. My friend, without hesitation selects the six of hearts. Now for the kill, I ask him to tell me how many cards he wants me to pull out of my pocket before I produce 'the card he has selected.' He calls for the fifth card and watches in astonishment as the fifth card is, in fact, the six of hearts.

PROPAGANDA

The A.L. Williams sales organization is adamant in its belief that cash value life insurance should be banished from the face of the earth. The sales force is reputed to be especially aggressive in its solicitation of customers and the sales pitch used to sell term insurance.

I had a personal experience with an A.L. Williams agent. This agent somehow got my name and showed up on my doorstep totally unannounced - no phone call for an appointment, no warning whatsoever. And believe me, there was no distortion about what she wanted to discuss. She wanted to talk about nothing but life insurance. She apparently didn't realize I was also in the life insurance business, and I didn't enlighten her. I asked her if it was her normal practice to simply show up on a customer's doorstep, and she told me that it was the method used by all of her colleagues. She immediately began describing the horrors of cash value life insurance and proudly told me of her most recent customer conquest. Ten years prior the customer had purchased a Northwestern Mutual participating whole life insurance policy, and she had succeeded in replacing it with term insurance. I asked if she had taken into account the Northwestern Mutual policy's dividends. In an almost chant like explanation, she informed me that dividends are not guaranteed and should not be taken into account. In fact, Northwestern Mutual is one of the premier life insurance companies whose dividends are among the strongest in the industry. The customer who had the Northwestern Mutual policy replaced was done a tremendous disservice.

This A.L. Williams agent, like many of her colleagues I believe, is unaware of the harm she does to consumers because of her very narrow perspective concerning life insurance.

On the other side of this indoctrination process are the agents who blindly recommend permanent or whole life insurance. I recall from my days with a Connecticut-based insurance company a fellow agent I shall refer to as Jake, whose wife was pregnant at the time. He announced to me one morning that he had just applied for a $25,000 whole life policy. I thought he should purchase a term policy for at least $250,000, considering his added responsibilities. Jake seemed perplexed and told me that our manager had strongly recommended the whole life policy for $25,000.

Later in the day I had a meeting with the manager and in passing asked him why he had recommended that Jake buy $25,000 of whole life when his needs were for a much larger policy. And because of the very large difference in premiums between term and whole life insurance, I thought he should be buying term insurance. The manager said I was right, but that he wanted Jake to make a commitment to whole life so he wouldn't waver when recommending it to customers. The indoctrination is pretty serious when a manager is willing to recommend substantial underinsurance to an agent to keep him focused on his mission. Of course, Jake, being the professional agent he believed himself to be, might have figured this out for himself.

Imagine the poor consumer caught in the cross fire between an A.L. Williams agent and an agent indoctrinated to sell permanent or whole life insurance. Like a stopped clock, which is right only twice a day, agents who have been so thoroughly indoctrinated are seldom right in their recommendations to potential buyers.

COMPANIES OFFERING LOW-LOAD POLICIES ON A DIRECT BASIS

Ameritas Life Insurance Corporation and USAA Life Insurance Company are the only life insurance companies currently offering low-load, no-commission term and universal life policies directly to consumers.

Ameritas Life Insurance Corporation (800/552-3553), a mutual company founded in 1887, was known as Bankers Life Nebraska until 1988. Mutual companies are owned by their policyholders.

They are rated A+ Superior by A.M. Best. This is Best's highest rating. Weiss Research, Inc. rates Ameritas A, ranking them the fifth strongest life insurance company in America. Their Standard & Poor's rating is AA, which is considered excellent.

Ameritas helped pioneer the concept of low-load insurance in 1983. The subsidiary organization, Ameritas Marketing Corporation, was formed in 1987 to provide assistance to both fee-based life insurance advisers who recommend Ameritas no-commission products to their clients, as well as consumers interested in purchasing these products directly.

In June 1991 Ameritas Marketing Corporation merged with Vest Insurance Marketing Corp., in Houston. The new name of their marketing unit for low-load life insurance policies is Veritas Corp.

All current premiums on both new and in-force Ameritas no- commission universal life policies receive a currently declared interest rate guaranteed for 12 months. After the initial 12 month guarantee, all no-commission universal life premiums receive a pooled renewal rate. This pooled renewal rate is guaranteed for one month. Below are the new money and the pooled renewal rates from June 1987 to December 1990:

	New Money	Renewal
6/87	8.50%	9.10%
10/87	8.75	9.10
1/88	8.75	9.75
3/88	8.50	9.50
6/88	8.50	9.25
9/88	8.75	9.25
10/88	8.75	9.00
7/89	8.50	8.75
8/89	8.25	8.75
3/90	8.50	8.75
4/90	8.50	8.55
9/90	8.50	8.30
12/90	8.25	8.30

Ameritas cost of insurance rates for no-commission policies are based on current company and industry experience, without projection for possible future improvements. Ameritas periodically reviews current mortality and expense experience and adjusts current rates when warranted. Ameritas did reduce the cost of insurance rate once since the policy form was introduced in 1986.

USAA, located in San Antonio, Texas, was founded in 1922. USAA members insure one another and share in any profits realized. Unlike other insurance products sold by USAA, which are only available to active and retired military officers, USAA's life insurance products are available to the general public. USAA began selling life insurance products to the general public in 1963.

They are rated A+ Superior by A.M. Best, their highest rating. USAA is rated A- by Weiss Research, Inc.. This is a very strong financial rating.

USAA universal life policies are credited with interest as declared by them. These rates are adjusted as often as each month. Below is a history of interest credited rates from June 1987 to December 1990:

	Interest Credited Rate		Interested Credited Rate
6/87	9.55%	4/88	8.90%
8/87	9.50%	3/89	9.00%
9/87	9.40%	10/89	8.90%
10/87	9.30%	12/89	8.80%
1/88	9.00%	10/90	8.75%

As is the case with Ameritas, USAA's cost of insurance rates are based on current company and industry experience, without projection for possible future improvements. USAA periodically reviews current mortality and expense experience and adjusts current cost of insurance rates as warranted.

LIFE INSURANCE RATES

THE ONLY PURPOSE OF THESE SCHEDULES IS FOR YOU TO DETERMINE WHETHER NO-COMMISSION TERM OR UNIVERSAL LIFE INSURANCE IS MOST APPROPRIATE FOR YOUR LIFE INSURANCE PURCHASE. THE FIRST STEP IS TO COMPARE THE COST OF TERM WITH THE COST OF UNIVERSAL LIFE. WHEN YOU HAVE DETERMINED THE TYPE OF LIFE INSURANCE YOU WISH TO PURCHASE, CONTACT AMERITAS, USAA OR BOTH TO OBTAIN PROPOSAL ILLUSTRATIONS FOR THE POLICY OR POLICIES YOU INTEND TO PURCHASE.

AMERITAS FIVE-YEAR LEVEL TERM - This policy was discussed in Chapter Six. Premium remains level for five years. Premium is guaranteed for three years. This policy can be purchased until age 65. It is renewable every five years, through age 80, without evidence of insurability. In order to review subsequent five-year premium rates you must contact Ameritas and request an illustration. The rates given in these tables are accurate for the first five-year period only. There are Preferred and Standard Non-Smoker rates and Standard Smoker rates. In order to qualify for the Preferred Non-smoker rate these guidelines must be met:

1. No tobacco use of any kind in the last 12 months;
2. No family history of death from heart disease, cardio-
    vascular impairments or diabetes prior to age 60;
3. Blood profile values should be favorable, including
    cholesterol, triglycerides and lipids;
4. No abnormal findings during urinalysis;

5. No history of or current treatment for high blood pressure, cancer, diabetes, mental or nervous disorders, or disorders of heart, lungs, liver or kidneys;
6. Height and weight must comply with established underwriting guidelines;
7. No driving convictions for reckless driving or driving under the influence of alcohol or drugs in the past five years.

If you meet or believe you could meet these guidelines, use the Preferred rate. To determine the premium for the first five years, multiply the rate per $1,000 by the number of $1,000 units you might consider buying. For example, the rate per $1,000 for a 38-year-old male preferred non-smoker is $1.17. If $600,000 of life insurance were being considered, the $1.17 is multiplied by 600, for a premium of $702. The rates in the schedule are based on purchasing $500,000 or more of life insurance. The actual rates for purchases of less than $500,000 are slightly higher. This policy may be purchased until age 65 and may be renewed until age 80.

ANNUAL PREMIUM RATES PER $1,000

Attained Age	Male			Female		
	Non-Smoker		Smoker	Non-Smoker		Smoker
	Preferred	Standard		Preferred	Standard	
20	.96	1.14	1.65	.80	.90	1.02
21	.96	1.14	1.65	.80	.90	1.02
22	.96	1.14	1.65	.80	.90	1.03
23	.96	1.14	1.65	.80	.90	1.03
24	.96	1.14	1.65	.80	.90	1.04
25	.96	1.14	1.65	.80	.90	1.04
26	.96	1.14	1.65	.80	.91	1.06
27	.96	1.14	1.65	.81	.92	1.09
28	.96	1.14	1.65	.82	.93	1.12
29	.96	1.14	1.67	.83	.95	1.15
30	.96	1.14	1.70	.84	.97	1.20
31	.97	1.15	1.75	.86	1.00	1.25
32	.98	1.16	1.81	.88	1.02	1.31
33	.99	1.18	1.89	.90	1.06	1.37
34	1.01	1.21	1.98	.93	1.10	1.45
35	1.04	1.25	2.09	.97	1.15	1.54
36	1.08	1.30	2.21	1.01	1.21	1.65
37	1.12	1.35	2.35	1.07	1.29	1.78
38	1.17	1.42	2.51	1.12	1.36	1.93
39	1.23	1.50	2.70	1.19	1.44	2.08
40	1.30	1.60	2.92	1.25	1.53	2.23
41	1.39	1.72	3.20	1.32	1.62	2.39
42	1.50	1.87	3.52	1.39	1.73	2.56
43	1.61	2.03	3.87	1.47	1.83	2.74
44	1.73	2.19	4.22	1.55	1.94	2.91
45	1.85	2.35	4.56	1.63	2.05	3.08
46	1.96	2.50	4.87	1.71	2.15	3.23
47	2.07	2.64	5.16	1.78	2.25	3.37
48	2.18	2.80	5.46	1.86	2.36	3.52
49	2.31	2.97	5.79	1.94	2.47	3.67
50	2.47	3.18	6.15	2.04	2.60	3.84
51	2.65	3.42	6.55	2.15	2.74	4.03
52	2.84	3.68	6.96	2.26	2.90	4.22
53	3.05	3.97	7.42	2.38	3.06	4.43
54	3.29	4.30	7.92	2.52	3.25	4.67
55	3.47	4.68	8.48	2.68	3.47	4.93
56	3.88	5.10	9.09	2.87	3.72	5.23
57	4.21	5.55	9.74	3.07	4.00	5.57
58	4.58	6.05	10.45	3.29	4.30	5.92
59	5.00	6.63	11.24	3.53	4.62	6.28
60	5.50	7.30	12.14	3.77	4.95	6.64
61	6.19	8.22	13.34	4.04	5.31	7.00
62	6.88	9.14	14.53	4.31	5.67	7.36
63	7.56	10.07	15.73	4.58	6.04	7.72
64	8.25	10.98	16.92	4.85	6.40	8.08
65	8.94	11.91	18.12	5.12	6.76	8.44

USAA ANNUAL RENEWAL TERM - This policy was discussed in Chapter Six. Premium rates go up each year. Rates are guaranteed for one year. During the past seven years this non-guaranteed rate has gone down twice. Policy is renewable to age 70 without evidence of insurability. These rates may be used to review the premium in the years ahead. It is recommended that you calculate the premium for a five-year period to compare it with the Ameritas' five-year level term policy. There are Standard Smoker and Non-Smoker rates. To determine your premium rate, multiply the rate per $1,000 by the number of $1,000 units being considered. Then add $30 to this figure. The $30 is a fixed policy fee. For example, a 38-year-old male non-smoker purchasing a $600,000 policy, would multiply $1.00 times 600, which is $600, and then add the policy fee of $30, for a total of $630. For five years, simply repeat this calculation for a male at ages 39, 40, 41 and 42.

The rate schedule is based on a purchase of $500,000 or more. For life insurance less than $500,000 the actual premium rate will be slightly higher.

ANNUAL PREMIUM RATES PER $1,000

Attained	Male		Female	
Age	Non-Smoker	Smoker	Non-Smoker	Smoker
20	.87	1.13	.76	1.12
21	.87	1.13	.76	1.12
22	.87	1.13	.76	1.12
23	.87	1.13	.76	1.12
24	.87	1.13	.76	1.12
25	.87	1.13	.76	1.12
26	.87	1.14	.76	1.13
27	.87	1.15	.76	1.14
28	.87	1.16	.76	1.14
29	.87	1.17	.77	1.15
30	.87	1.19	.77	1.17
31	.87	1.21	.77	1.18
32	.87	1.25	.78	1.21
33	.88	1.30	.80	1.24

Attained	Male		Female	
Age	Non-Smoker	Smoker	Non-Smoker	Smoker
34	.88	1.37	.82	1.29
35	.92	1.46	.85	1.35
36	.94	1.56	.88	1.41
37	.96	1.66	.92	1.48
38	1.00	1.78	.96	1.54
39	1.05	1.90	1.00	1.61
40	1.11	2.04	1.05	1.69
41	1.18	2.20	1.10	1.79
42	1.25	2.39	1.15	1.92
43	1.34	2.61	1.22	2.07
44	1.46	2.87	1.29	2.25
45	1.61	3.17	1.40	2.45
46	1.82	3.48	1.51	2.68
47	2.08	3.78	1.60	2.91
48	2.37	4.08	1.69	3.13
49	2.66	4.40	1.80	3.38
50	2.93	4.77	1.92	3.66
51	3.14	5.20	2.07	3.99
52	3.32	5.72	2.26	4.39
53	3.50	6.33	2.48	4.86
54	3.69	7.06	2.75	5.41
55	3.92	7.93	3.08	6.08
56	4.16	8.78	3.40	6.74
57	4.39	9.49	3.67	7.30
58	4.68	10.17	3.93	7.83
59	5.10	10.91	4.22	8.39
60	5.74	11.81	4.57	9.09
61	6.59	12.97	5.01	9.99
62	7.59	14.47	5.59	11.10
63	8.77	16.43	6.34	12.28
64	10.13	18.93	7.31	13.52
65	11.69	22.07	8.53	14.79
66	13.46	25.00	9.66	16.24
67	15.47	27.81	10.87	17.81
68	17.70	30.30	12.23	19.32
69	20.20	33.00	13.85	21.42

USAA SEVEN-YEAR TERM - This policy was discussed in Chapter Fifteen. Annual premium increases each year. Policy can only be renewed for seven years, after which time the policy is canceled. To continue this policy for more than seven years the insured would have to prove he were still insurable. This policy should only be used for term life insurance needs of short duration.

To calculate the premium, multiply the rate per $1,000 by the number of $1,000 units being purchased and add $30 to this figure.

ANNUAL PREMIUM RATES PER $1,000

Issue Age	Male Non-Smoker	Smoker	Female Non-Smoker	Smoker
20	.83	1.05	.80	1.03
21	.83	1.05	.80	1.03
22	.83	1.05	.80	1.03
23	.83	1.05	.80	1.03
24	.83	1.05	.80	1.03
25	.83	1.05	.80	1.03
26	.83	1.06	.80	1.04
27	.83	1.06	.80	1.04
28	.83	1.07	.80	1.05
29	.83	1.16	.80	1.14
30	.85	1.29	.81	1.23
31	.87	1.38	.84	1.31
32	.89	1.39	.86	1.33
33	.90	1.39	.88	1.36
34	.91	1.42	.89	1.40
35	.93	1.53	.92	1.44
36	.96	1.67	.93	1.50
37	.98	1.82	.93	1.62
38	1.00	1.98	.94	1.76
39	1.03	2.11	.95	1.88
40	1.08	2.25	.98	1.94
41	1.16	2.36	1.03	1.99
42	1.25	2.48	1.09	2.06
43	1.36	2.58	1.16	2.11
44	1.48	2.70	1.23	2.18

Issue	Male		Female	
Age	Non-Smoker	Smoker	Non-Smoker	Smoker
45	1.59	3.84	1.31	2.27
46	1.69	3.01	1.38	2.38
47	1.79	3.21	1.46	2.63
48	1.89	3.42	1.53	2.86
49	2.01	3.65	1.62	3.02
50	2.14	3.92	1.72	3.24
51	2.28	4.25	1.83	3.42
52	2.43	4.62	1.93	3.70
53	2.59	5.07	2.06	3.96
54	2.79	5.40	2.20	4.22
55	3.03	5.73	2.38	4.43
56	3.30	5.97	2.58	4.72
57	3.60	6.20	2.80	4.99
58	3.93	6.45	3.04	5.24
59	4.33	7.01	3.34	5.50
60	4.81	7.85	3.70	5.81
61	5.38	8.89	4.11	6.27
62	6.01	9.98	4.57	6.89
63	6.72	10.75	5.09	7.70
64	7.48	10.98	5.68	8.66
65	8.25	11.47	6.35	9.71

AMERITAS UNIVERSAL LIFE - This policy was discussed in Chapter Seven. This rate schedule is only provided so that you can determine the approximate annual premium cost for this universal life policy. Target premium rate is based on a policy that endows at age 95 (cash value and death benefit are approximately equal at age 95), assuming current cost of insurance rates and an interest credited assumption of 8.0%. If a no-commission universal life policy is being considered, you must contact Ameritas, USAA or both and request proposal illustrations.

To determine the approximate annual premium cost for Ameritas no-commission universal life, multiply the rate per $1,000 by the number of $1,000 units being considered.

ANNUAL PREMIUM RATES PER $1,000

Attained	Male		Female	
Age	Non-Smoker	Smoker	Non-Smoker	Smoker
20	1.93	3.04	1.51	2.03
21	1.98	3.14	1.56	2.12
22	2.05	3.24	1.61	2.20
23	2.12	3.34	1.67	2.30
24	2.20	3.46	1.73	2.41
25	2.28	3.60	1.80	2.52
26	2.38	3.76	1.89	2.66
27	2.49	3.94	1.97	2.80
28	2.60	4.14	2.06	2.95
29	2.74	4.35	2.18	3.11
30	2.89	4.58	2.30	3.30
31	3.06	4.82	2.42	3.48
32	3.24	5.07	2.57	3.68
33	3.45	5.34	2.73	3.90
34	3.68	5.64	2.90	4.14
35	3.92	5.97	3.08	4.39
36	4.18	6.34	3.28	4.65
37	4.64	6.74	3.49	4.93
38	4.78	7.16	3.72	5.23
39	5.01	7.62	3.96	5.54
40	5.45	8.11	4.21	5.87
41	5.82	8.62	4.48	6.22

Attained	Male		Female	
Age	Non-Smoker	Smoker	Non-Smoker	Smoker
42	6.22	9.15	4.77	6.58
43	6.64	9.72	5.08	6.97
44	7.09	10.32	5.40	7.38
45	7.57	10.96	5.75	7.81
46	8.08	11.64	6.10	8.26
47	8.61	12.37	6.48	8.73
48	9.17	13.14	6.87	9.23
49	9.77	13.94	7.30	9.76
50	10.41	14.78	7.78	10.32
51	11.10	15.64	8.31	10.92
52	11.82	16.54	8.89	11.54
53	12.59	17.49	9.51	12.20
54	13.42	18.51	10.17	12.91
55	14.32	19.62	10.89	13.70
56	15.27	20.85	11.65	14.57
57	16.28	22.18	12.46	15.48
58	17.35	23.59	13.33	16.47
59	18.50	25.02	14.26	17.51
60	19.77	26.47	15.26	18.62
61	21.16	27.90	16.31	19.74
62	22.63	29.35	17.42	20.91
63	24.28	30.87	18.62	22.15
64	26.10	32.54	19.94	23.53
65	28.10	34.42	21.37	25.09
66	30.32	36.54	22.93	26.81
67	32.72	38.84	24.58	28.67
68	35.28	41.32	26.38	30.69
69	37.96	43.98	28.35	32.88
70	40.76	46.80	30.53	35.31
71	42.94	49.32	31.39	37.13
72	46.09	52.08	33.76	40.38
73	49.46	55.01	36.33	43.88
74	53.00	58.38	39.18	47.52
75	56.89	62.23	42.40	51.25
76	61.58	67.39	46.63	55.25
77	66.33	72.59	50.96	59.32
78	71.18	77.92	55.73	63.60
79	76.70	83.95	60.37	68.12
80	82.00	89.95	65.53	72.93

APPENDIX F

HAZARDOUS TERM INSURANCE PRICING STRATEGIES

There are pricing strategies used by some life insurance companies selling term insurance that appear very attractive to potential buyers, but in reality aren't a very good buy when compared with the no-commission term insurance policies sold directly by Ameritas and USAA.

A pricing strategy used by some insurance companies is to price their term insurance policies very low for a year or two, with substantial annual increases thereafter. Exhibit F-1 demonstrates this first-year low-ball strategy compared to USAA's no-commission annual renewal term policy for a 38-year-old male non-smoker. These premium rates are based on a policy for $600,000 with standard non-smoker rates:

EXHIBIT F-1		
INSURANCE AMOUNT: $600,000		MALE 38, NON-SMOKER STANDARD
Age	Connecticut Based Company*	USAA**
38	$560	$630
39	710	660
40	854	696
41	1,004	738
42	1,148	780
43	1,310	834
44	1,472	906
45	1,628	996
46	1,790	1,122
47	1,946	1,278
Total	$12,422	$8,640

* Rate guaranteed for 10 years.
** USAA rate guaranteed for first year only. Non-guaranteed rates have been decreased twice during the seven years this policy has been sold.

The low-ball rate in the first year for the Connecticut-based company term policy compared to the USAA policy could entice some consumers to buy it rather than the USAA policy because many consumers don't consider the renewal premiums.

This first-year low-ball pricing is the primary reason I haven't included a term insurance rate chart for various companies. Such a rate chart would be misleading because it wouldn't disclose the differences in renewal premiums, which are more important than differences in the initial premium.

Another popular pricing strategy is to offer a low premium rate for a specified period of time, for example five years. Then beginning in the sixth year, low rates would continue if the insured can prove he is in the same health as when the policy was originally purchased. If the insured isn't in the same good health at the specified time, the premium rates would go up substantially. These policies are known as re-entry policies. Exhibit F-2 provides an example of a re-entry policy with and without re-entry. That is, the first column assumes the insured is able to re-enter because his health condition is the same. The second column assumes the insured is unable to qualify for the better premiums because of poorer health at re-entry time. This re-entry policy sold by an Ohio-based insurance company is compared with a no-commission term policy sold by Ameritas. Both are five-year level term policies. The Ameritas policy doesn't require re-entry. These illustrations are for a 38-year-old, non-smoking male for $600,000. The rates are for a preferred non-smoker:

EXHIBIT F-2

INSURANCE AMOUNT: $600,000   MALE 38, NON-SMOKER

| | Ohio Based Company* | | PREFERRED |
Age	With Re-Entry	W/O Re-Entry	Ameritas**
38	$776	N/A	$702
39	"	"	"
40	"	"	"
41	"	"	"
42			
43	950	$1,550†	965
44	"	1,724	"
45	"	1,922	"
46	"	2,144	"
47	"	2,390	"
Total	$8,630	$13,610	$8,330

* Rate guaranteed during initial five-year period and subsequent five years for re-entry only.
** Ameritas rate is guaranteed for three years. Policy doesn't require re-entry.
† Rate if insured does not qualify for re-entry due to health condition. This rate is not guaranteed.

Re-entry policies are a good buy if the insured is able to re-enter at specified times. If the insured isn't able to re-enter, these policies become very expensive. Since it is not possible to know in advance which insureds will qualify for re-entry and which won't, these policies are too unpredictable.

LIFE INSURANCE AS AN INVESTMENT: REALITY OR FICTION

Life insurance company home-office personnel and agents in the field spend a good deal of time dreaming up exotic investment schemes into which they can fit their life insurance policies. They will search through the tax codes to find presumed loopholes that can be used to give their life insurance policies an advantage over more conventional investments. Any investment where the contribution is tax deductible, such as an IRA, has inherent advantages over non-deductible investments. With the exception of employer-provided group life insurance and life insurance that is required in a divorce settlement, life insurance premiums are never tax deductible. But this hasn't stopped insurance people from trying to develop life insurance investment plans they claim allow for tax-deductible premiums.

I was recently hired by a client who owns a medium-sized company. He had been solicited by an agent offering him a life insurance investment plan that featured tax-deductible premiums. The client retained my services to determine whether this claim was valid.

The plan was presented in a 16-page booklet. One of the claims made was that, while many other companies had tried, they were the only company that had succeeded in designing such a plan. This should tell us something. The booklet, in stunning detail, explained the logic and supporting tax laws proving that the tax-deductible premium was legitimate. The plan was very complicated, so I won't describe it to you in detail except to point out that the starting point for this exotic scheme was a paper transaction in which the policyowner borrows the first-year premium (up to $50,000) from the insurance company. This borrowing is permitted, according to the booklet, up to its premium commitment. How do you borrow against a commitment? The paper transaction policy loan is used to justify taking tax deductions for the interest paid for the loan. The insurance company charges 15% interest. Under current tax law, a tax deduction is permitted for corporations for interest payments on policy loans, up to a maximum of $50,000.

Unfortunately, the tax courts have been consistent in disallowing interest deductions on loans that are considered "sham" transactions - that is, transactions offering the taxpayer nothing of economic substance other than the hoped-for deduction. It is my opinion that this plan's promised tax-deductible premium is based on a "sham" transaction and the taxpayer would be denied the interest tax deduction.

However, in the complicated arena of tax law, opinions vary because a specific transaction may not have been specifically addressed by tax regulations or tax court cases. Tax advisers can only look for transactions similar to the one being reviewed and guess how the tax laws would apply to the untested transaction. I am sure there are prudent tax advisers who may offer an opinion different from mine, especially if they are being paid by a company setting up such a plan.

But regardless of whether this plan is legitimate, the basic value of the life insurance policy funding this plan isn't very good. There are many other life insurance policies that are a much better buy. This is the magician aspect characteristic of some life insurance selling. The consumer is distracted by the promise of a tax-deductible premium (or some other gimmick) and the basics of the policy are ignored.

Even more basic, my client had no objective need for the additional life insurance. His only interest in this plan was the investment potential.

Consumers, particularly medium-sized business owners, all across this great land of ours are aggressively pressured by agents to believe stories similar to the one above. Investment programs that sound to good to be true should be avoided - especially if they involve the purchase of life insurance.

Appendix H

Agent Confusion

I write a life insurance column for the American Association of Individual Investors (AAII) Journal. In my April 1990 column I mentioned that universal life is a permanent form of life insurance. This prompted two letters challenging my comment. They were printed in the August 1990 *AAII Journal* along with my reply. These letters, reprinted on pages 164 and 165, will help you understand the confusion that exists concerning the various forms of permanent life insurance and the damage this confusion can cause to consumers who are trying to evaluate the most appropriate form of life insurance for their needs.

Letters

Life Insurance: Adding to the Agenda. . .

To the Editor:

The article in the April 1990 issue entitled "Taking Control of the Life Insurance Agenda" was an excellent one giving some basic facts and advice concerning life insurance. I would like to add a few more points for the benefit of the readers.

Before buying life insurance, one has to keep in mind the fact that life insurance becomes costlier the older you become. Hence, a person 50 years old would end up paying much higher premiums than a person 25 years old. At the age of 50, a person may find a better choice by investing elsewhere. For additional security, he may opt for an accident policy rather than life insurance. Generally, premiums on accident policies do not have any link to age group.

Life insurance is primarily a miracle of compound interest. If you are able to achieve compounding of interest through some other method, you may be able to find a better choice. One important point to consider is whether to buy life insurance from mutual or participating companies (owned by the policy holders) or from stock or nonparticipating companies (owned by the stockholders). On a long-term basis, the participating companies have offered better returns to policy holders.

Waiver clause is another important factor to be considered, especially for elderly people.

A.W. Nagda
Atlanta, Georgia

. . .And Critiquing It

To the Editor:

The article "Taking Control of the Life Insurance Agenda" in your April 1990 issue contains a very misleading concept that many insurance purchasers unexpectedly fall victim to. Caveat emptor (let the buyer beware) that life insurance is not permanent insurance, i.e., it is not whole life according to traditional life insurance terminology (whole life insurance in the context of a guaranteed premium for a guaranteed death benefit and guaranteed cash value). All universal life policies I have examined contain "term insurance" inside the contract that is bought up by the "investment pool" remaining available after expenses and mortality charges are deducted from that investment pool. This inside term insurance has a target cost and a maximum premium cost, which may be charged if the mortality experience of the company does not match current mortality charges illustrated. The fact that the insurance purchaser may run out of life insurance, cash value, or both, if mortality charges increase or investment results decrease is an inherent risk in these policies. The universal policy owner must either increase his premium payments or experience reduced insurance protection under this scenario. Universal life is not a panacea to reduced insurance cost without a corresponding increase in risk to the buyer. I am not implying that universal life insurance is inherently a bad buy (although that point could be argued convincingly); however, it is fundamentally incorrect to refer to it as permanent insurance protection.

Keith M. Duhe, CFP
Northwestern Mutual Life

To the Editor:

I was amazed that Peter Katt (in "Taking Control of the Life Insurance Agenda") would quote Joseph Belth concerning apathy, lack of knowledge and inherent complexity and then call universal life permanent insurance. Mr. Belth has criticized universal life in his newsletters. My question is: How can permanent insurance be equated to current (non-guaranteed) interest and mortality assumptions? I would think permanent and guaranteed would be the answer, especially when you are talking about *life* insurance.

John Cheek
Orlando, Florida

Peter Katt replies: Will the real permanent form of life insurance please stand up! To claim that whole life policies are the only true form of permanent insurance is a partisan argument that doesn't add much to the debate. The two letters make the point that whole life policies have guaranteed premiums, cash value and death benefit while universal life policies' current interest credited rates and cost of insurance rates aren't guaranteed. What they fail to mention is that participating whole life policies, in order to be competitive with other alternatives, are dependent on the non-guaranteed dividends. And other forms of whole life policies are dependent on non-guaranteed interest-sensitive formulations. They also fail to mention that universal life policies have guaranteed interest credited rates and cost of insurance rates.

The fact is, if participating whole life policies failed to pay dividends or if universal life policies began crediting guaranteed interest and charging maximum rates for cost of insurance, our world would have become so bad that life insurance may be the least important item in our lives. To compare permanent forms of life insurance based on their bottom line guarantees is irrelevant.

The criticism of universal life by Joseph Belth and others is based on agents providing illustrations that assume rates of interest that are too high or companies that factor into their illustration systems improving mortality in the future that is not justified. But these criticisms should not be limited to universal life policies. They are true for participating and interest-sensitive whole life policies as well.

The issue addressed by Joseph Belth and others really involves the imprudent designs of various forms of permanent life insurance for competitive purposes.

Universal life, fueled by the high interest rates in the early 1980s, produced a competitive response from insurance companies with more traditional forms of permanent insurance, which resulted in the lowering of premiums and raising of cash values. But these redesigns were based on non-guaranteed dividends or interest-sensitive formulations.

With inflation and interest rates much lower now, many permanent life insurance policies (universal and whole life policies alike) are not performing as projected when they were sold. The real problem is the failure of life insurance agents to adequately monitor the policies they sold and to inform their customers of changes in interest credited rates, cost of insurance rates and dividends that adversely affect the policy they purchased.

The issue that your readers do not mention is the recommendation that astute consumers purchase no-commission universal life policies on a direct basis. The future value of any permanent life insurance policy is dependent on three factors: mortality experience; investment results; and expenses. A full-commission permanent life insurance policy has first-year acquisition expenses of approximately 135% of the first-year premium (which primarily is the commissions paid to the agent and the general agent), compared with first-year acquisition expenses for no-commission universal life policies of approximately 15%.

And subsequent expenses are substantially lower for no-commission universal life policies.

If there were other forms of permanent life insurance available on a no-commission basis from highly-rated insurance companies, they would also be recommended.

INDEX

FAMILY PROTECTION LIFE INSURANCE CALCULATION WORKSHEET
FOR THE PRIMARY INCOME EARNER

STEP 1:

Decide the amount of monthly income, on a pretax basis, your family will need if you are deceased_____ (line 1). This is the survivor's monthly income goal.

STEP 2:

Subtract from the amount in line 1 income, on a monthly basis, available to meet this survivor's monthly income goal.

Surviving spouse's monthly income	_____
Social Security (dependent children or other categories)	_____
Pension benefits payable	_____
Other	
	_____
	_____
	_____
	_____

Total	(line 2)	_____

(Note: You may wish to ignore any or all of these income sources to provide your survivors with more income and therefore, more flexibility. Cross out sources of monthly income you don't wish to consider.)

Subtract from line 1		_____
Amount on line 2		_____
Survivor's Monthly Income Goal	(line 3)	_____

STEP 3:

To express the survivor's monthly income goal on an annual basis, multiply line 3 by 12.

	(line 3)	_____
		x 12
Survivor's Annual Income Goal	(line 4)	_____

STEP 4:

Select an assumed investment rate of return on a pretax basis.

	(line 5)	_____

Move the decimal point for the assumed investment rate in line 5 two places to the left.

	(line 6)	_____

Divide line 4 by line 6.

_____ divided by _____ = (line 7) _____

The result in line 7 is the Survivor's Principal Goal.

Step 5:

If you wish to provide additional funding for future inflation you may increase the survivor's principal goal from line 9 by some percentage - 10%, 20%, 30% etc. This may not be necessary because principal could be used for additional support if needed. Also if you review your family protection needs every two years this will tend to offset the need to estimate future inflation.

Survivor's Principal Goal	(line 7)	_____
Inflation factor		x 1.__
(For example, 20% would be 1.20)		
Survivor's Principal Goal	(line 8)	_____

Step 6:

List financial obligations you would like to fund. (Note: Obligations such as mortgages, which are being paid off with monthly payments, may not need additional funding if your survivor's monthly income goal will cover these monthly payments. Obligations such as college education for children may be expressed either in present value dollars or at their estimated future value.)

College education fund		_____
Other		
		_____
		_____
		_____
		_____
Total	(line 9)	_____
Add line 9 and		_____
line 8		_____
Survivor's Principal Goal	(line 10)	_____

Step 7:

Reduce the survivor's principal goal by assets presently available to fund this goal.

Life insurance   _____
Vested pension funds   _____
Personal investments   _____
Other

                                       _____
                                       _____
                                       _____
                                       _____

Total   (line 11) _____
Subtract from line 10   _____
amount on line 11   _____

Survivor's Principal Goal Deficit   _____

This is a 'rough estimate' of the amount of life insurance that should be purchased for the primary income earner. To further simplify this process, skip steps 2, 5 and 6.

FAMILY PROTECTION LIFE INSURANCE CALCULATION WORKSHEET
FOR PRIMARY INCOME EARNER'S SPOUSE

STEP 1:

Decide the amount of monthly income, on a pretax basis, that would be lost if the primary income earner's spouse were deceased.

                                (line 1) _____

Determine the additional monthly expenses that would be incurred if the primary income earner's spouse were deceased.

                                (line 2) _____

Add lines 1 and 2.

        Survivor's Monthly Income Goal (line 3) _____

STEP 2:

To express the survivor's monthly income goal on an annual basis, multiply line 3 by 12.

                                (line 3) _____
                                            x12

        Survivor's Annual Income Goal   (line 4) _____

STEP 3:

Select an assumed investment rate of return, on a pretax basis.

(line 5) _____

Move the decimal point for the assumed investment rate in line 5 two places to the left.   (line 6) _____

Divide line 4 by line 6.

_____ divided by _____ = (line 7) _____

The result on line 7 is the survivor's principal goal.

STEP 4:

Reduce the survivor's principal goal by assets presently available to fund this goal.

Life insurance	_____
Pension funds	_____
Personal investments	_____
Other	
	_____
	_____
	_____
	_____
Total (line 8)	_____
Subtract from line 7 amount on line 8	_____
	_____
Survivor's Principal Goal Deficit	_____

This is a 'rough estimate' of life insurance that should be purchased for the primary income earner's spouse.

The Life Insurance Fiasco: How to Avoid It may be
ordered from Publishers Distribution Service
by calling 1-800-345-0096 (toll free)

or 1-616-929-0733
(in Michigan and outside the U. S.)

or by FAX 1-616-929-3808

or by writing to:

Publishers Distribution Service
121 East Front Street, Suite 203
Traverse City, Michigan 49684

Visa and MasterCard accepted
Quantity discounts are available

Notes

Notes